The Control of Chemical and Biological Weapons

CARNEGIE ENDOWMENT FOR INTERNATIONAL PEACE
NEW YORK / 1971

Authors

Archibald S. Alexander

Former assistant director, U.S. Arms Control and Disarmament Agency; former Under-Secretary of the Army.

R. R. Baxter

Professor, Law School, Harvard University.

Stewart Blumenfeld

Ph.D. candidate, School of Public Health, University of California at Los Angeles.

David Brown

1969–1970 Fellow of the John F. Kennedy School of Public Administration, Harvard University.

Thomas Buergenthal

Professor, Faculty of Law and Jurisprudence, State University of New York at Buffalo.

Matthew Meselson

Professor, The Biological Laboratories, Harvard University; leader of the American Association for the Advancement of Science team surveying the ecological effects of the use of herbicides in Vietnam.

© *Carnegie Endowment for International Peace 1971*

Library of Congress Catalog Card Number: 73–151279

PREFACE

In November 1969, President Richard Nixon enunciated new United States policies in the field of chemical and biological warfare (CBW). These called for the resubmission of the 1925 Geneva Protocol to the U.S. Senate for ratification, renunciation of the use of biological weapons, and limitation of United States programs thereon to strictly defensive purposes. The President further recommended that additional measures to limit CBW be negotiated at the Conference of the Committee on Disarmament (CCD) in Geneva.

In the winter of 1970 the Carnegie Endowment for International Peace initiated a project within its arms control program to study some of the central issues that might arise in implementing these policies and in attempting to control chemical and biological warfare. Four papers were prepared to illuminate key problem areas. The first, by Richard R. Baxter and Thomas Buergenthal, involves an analysis of the legal aspects of the Geneva Protocol; the second, by David Brown, and the third, by Stewart Blumenfeld and Matthew Meselson, examine the military value and political implications of the use of herbicides and riot control agents in warfare; and the fourth, by Archibald S. Alexander, reviews possible limitations on CBW going beyond the U.S. ratification of the Geneva Protocol. All four papers were discussed by an advisory group of legal, retired military, scientific, and international political experts assembled by the Endowment. Several government officials also attended the meetings of the group as observers. The advisory group comprised the following persons:

William Bader—Ford Foundation
Dr. Ivan Bennett—New York University Medical School

The authors met with the advisory group and observers on three separate occasions and had the benefit of their comments in the preparation of the final versions of their papers. However, the authors alone are responsible for the views expressed. The brief personal comments of some members of the group on the issues involved appear as an annex to the prepared papers. The Endowment assumes full responsibility for the decision to publish the papers together with these comments and is grateful to the authors, the members of the advisory group, and government observers for their participation in this project.

Joseph E. Johnson
*President, Carnegie Endowment
for International Peace*

December 1970

CONTENTS

LEGAL ASPECTS OF THE
GENEVA PROTOCOL OF 1925

by R. R. Baxter and Thomas Buergenthal

In his policy statement of 25 November 1969, on chemical and biological warfare, President Richard M. Nixon declared that the Administration would ask the Senate for advice and consent to the ratification of the Geneva Protocol of 1925. At the same time, the President reaffirmed the renunciation by the United States of "the first use of lethal chemical weapons" and extended "this renunciation to the first use of incapacitating chemicals." With regard to biological weapons, the President renounced the use of all biological weapons and methods of warfare; declared that the United States would confine its biological research to defensive measures; and ordered the Defense Department to make recommendations for the "disposal of existing stocks of bacteriological weapons." On 14 February 1970, the President extended the ban on biological weapons to include toxins.*

Crucial to any meaningful assessment of present or future United States policy in this field is an understanding of the

---

* Subsequently to the completion of this paper, the President of the United States on 19 August 1970 transmitted the Geneva Protocol of 1925 to the Senate for its approval. In the report of the Secretary of State, which was transmitted with the President's letter, the Secretary of State proposed a reservation asserting the right of the United States to use chemical weapons in retaliation against an enemy state failing to observe the obligations laid down in the Protocol and explained that it is the understanding of the United States that the Protocol "does not prohibit the use in war of riot-control agents and chemical herbicides." [U.S. Dept. of State *Bulletin*, Vol. 273 (1970), p. 63.]

The Senate may, of course, make its own determinations about reservations and understandings with respect to a treaty submitted to it.

legal scope of the Geneva Protocol. This paper will accordingly describe the obligations the Protocol imposes, what steps the United States will have to take if it decides to become a party to the Protocol without accepting all of its obligations, and what legal problems it will encounter in doing so.

The Prohibitory Scope
of the Geneva Protocol of 1925

The Protocol for the Prohibition of the Use in War of Asphyxiating, Poisonous or Other Gases, and of Bacteriological Methods of Warfare was signed at Geneva on 17 June 1925.[1] It has been formally ratified by or is otherwise binding upon eighty-five nations,[2] including all the major military and industrial nations of the world except for the United States. Although the United States government participated in the drafting of the Geneva Protocol and signed it,[3] the Senate failed to give its consent to the ratification of the treaty.[4]

The Geneva Protocol prohibits two things: (a) "the use in war of asphyxiating, poisonous or other gases, and of all analogous liquids, materials or devices," and (b) "the use of bacteriological methods of warfare." It does not prohibit the production, acquisition, or stockpiling of these weapons, nor does it apply to their use for purposes other than in "war." This means, among other things, that the testing of these weapons is not proscribed by the Geneva Protocol; the same is true of the manufacture of equipment capable of dispersing them.

The major question that has arisen with regard to the interpretation of the Protocol is whether irritant chemicals (tear gas) and anti-plant chemicals fall within the prohibition of the use in war of "asphyxiating, poisonous or other gases." Before that question can be answered, we must be clear about the manner in which the meaning of a doubtful passage in a treaty is determined.

Treaties are to be interpreted "in accordance with the ordinary meaning to be given to the terms of the treaty in their context and in the light of its object and purpose."[5] There may also be taken into account the subsequent practices of the parties establishing their agreement on its interpretation.[6] And if the meaning of the agreement is still ambiguous or obscure, one may turn to the preparatory work of the treaty and the circumstances of its conclusion.[7]

It is important to notice in this connection that it is the subsequent practice of the parties that may be taken into account. This suggests that the interpretation attached to the Protocol by the United States, a non-party, carries much less weight than some have assumed. A certain amount of confusion has been occasioned by a failure to distinguish evidence that goes to the interpretation of the Protocol from evidence of the state of customary international law. The reach of the treaty prohibition of chemical warfare is not necessarily coextensive with the corresponding prohibition found in customary international law. In other words, it may well be that the Geneva Protocol—the treaty or conventional prohibition—outlaws all forms of chemical warfare, including irritant chemicals and anti-plant chemicals. This does not mean, however, that as sweeping a prohibition need necessarily have passed into customary international law as a rule binding on all states, whether or not parties to the Protocol.

Unless one recognizes that the reach of the conventional and the customary international law[8] rules need not be identical, it is impossible to determine from the available negotiating history and subsequent practice what forms of chemical warfare the Geneva Protocol was intended to outlaw. For what might be regarded as legally conclusive evidence to support a sweeping interpretation of the Geneva Protocol can, and in fact does, become much less conclusive for purposes of ascertaining the full scope of the customary rule. Thus, although the chemical warfare practice and declarations of states not parties to the Geneva Protocol are relevant evidence for the purpose of delimiting the scope of the customary rule, they do not bear witness to the scope of the conventional rule. If one is guided by this principle in analyzing the chemical warfare prohibition of the Geneva Protocol, many of the doubts regarding its intended scope disappear.

A. Irritant Chemicals

The prohibition of the Protocol that deals with chemical warfare is self-explanatory, at least to the extent that it outlaws the use of "asphyxiating" and "poisonous" gases and "all analogous liquids, materials or devices." The doubt as to the full scope of the prohibition, which in its English text—"or other gases"—could hardly have been expressed in more sweeping and all-embracing language, results from the fact that the French text of the Protocol[9] speaks of "gaz asphyxiantes, toxiques ou similaires." On the debatable premise that the use of the word "similaires" in the French text limits the prohibitory scope of the Protocol,[10] it has been suggested that the Protocol applies only to chemical agents having harmful consequences similar to those of asphyxiating or poisonous gases.[11] Leaving aside the question whether this restrictive interpretation is scientifically or medically meaningful, particularly when applied to the military uses of chemicals, the fact remains that the slight difference between the English and French texts of the Protocol has been used to support the argument that certain chemical weapons, such as tear gas and herbicides, do not come within the prohibition of the Protocol. Relying on this textual ambiguity, the United States government has argued that "it would be unreasonable to contend that any rule of international law prohibits the use in combat against an enemy, for humanitarian purposes, of agents that Governments around the world commonly use to control riots by their own people."[12] Similar contentions have been made with regard to the use in war of anti-plant chemicals.

1. *The history of the chemical warfare prohibition in the Geneva Protocol.* The language in which the Geneva Protocol proscribes the use of chemical weapons is found in a number of earlier treaties.[13] These attempts to outlaw chemical warfare reflected the abhorrence and outrage with which the international community reacted to the use of gas in the First World War. Among the different gases used by both sides in that war were various types of lachrymatory (tear) gases.[14] The massive use of lachrymators—it is estimated that 12,000 tons of this gas were employed—suggests that the draftsmen

of these treaties were well aware of the military uses of irritant chemicals.

(*a*) The Treaty of Versailles. The first international treaty to use the terminology employed in the Geneva Protocol was the Treaty of Versailles.[15] It provided in Article 171 that "the use of asphyxiating, poisonous or *other* gases and all analogous liquids, materials or devices being prohibited, their manufacture and importation are strictly forbidden in Germany." (Emphasis supplied.) The French text of Article 171 used the word "similaires," which is also true of all subsequent treaties that adopt the formula found in the Geneva Protocol. What meaning the draftsmen of the Versailles Treaty attached to this formula is not clear,[16] because they did not discuss its meaning. That little significance can be attached to the slight divergence between the English and French texts of Article 171 is apparent, moreover, from the language of Article 172 of the Treaty. It required Germany to disclose to the allies "the nature and mode of all explosives, toxic substances or other *like* chemical preparations used by them in the war. . . ." The French text of Article 172 renders the more restrictive "or other like chemical preparations" simply as "ou *autres* préparations chemiques."

(*b*) Treaty on Submarine and Gas Warfare. The Treaty on the Use of Submarines and Noxious Gases in Warfare, signed in Washington in 1922 by France, Great Britain, Italy, Japan, and the United States,[17] provided in Article 5 that:

> The use in war of asphyxiating, poisonous or other gases, and all analogous liquids, materials or devices, having been justly condemned by the general opinion of the civilized world and a prohibition of such use having been declared in treaties to which a majority of the civilized Powers are parties,
>
> The Signatory Powers, to the end that this prohibition shall be universally accepted as a part of international law binding alike the conscience and practice of nations, declare their assent to such prohibition, agree to be bound thereby as between themselves and invite all other civilized nations to adhere thereto.

Although the Treaty of Washington never entered into force because France failed to ratify it, it was ratified by the

United States. Most of the discussion in the Senate debate on the treaty related to submarine warfare and the question whether chemical weapons were more or less humane than other weapons.[18] The only discussion concerning the nature of the prohibition laid down in Article 5 consisted of the following exchange between Senator James Wadsworth, Jr. and Senator Henry Cabot Lodge:

> Mr. Wadsworth: . . . I think article 5 is drawn somewhat carelessly. . . . The phrase "other gases" is all inclusive. It reads: "asphyxiating, poisonous, or other gases."
>
> Mr. Lodge: To be used in war.
>
> Mr. Wadsworth: Yes; but there are gases used in war other than asphyxiating or poisonous gases.
>
> Mr. Townsend: What for?
>
> Mr. Wadsworth: For balloons, such as helium gas, and hydrogen. A strict construction would seem to prevent the use of any gas in war. Undoubtedly that is not meant. . . .
> It would seem in the French text that the word "similaires" ties the matter up, but in the English text the equivalent of "similaires" is not used. That, however, is a point of comparatively small importance.[19]

As his remarks indicate, Senator Wadsworth was concerned lest the language of Article 5 be construed to apply not only to the use of gas as a weapon, but to any use of gas in war whatsoever. But neither he nor any other Senator inquired whether Article 5 prohibited the use of tear gas or any other irritant chemical. This is particularly noteworthy because the documents of the conference at which the treaty was drafted, and which were before the Senate,[20] indicate that this question had been considered but had not been unequivocally resolved.[21]

The proposal to include in the Treaty of Washington a provision relating to chemical warfare came from the United States delegation, which was led by Secretary of State Charles Evans Hughes and included Senator Elihu Root. The deliberation on this agenda item took place in the Committee on Limitation of Armaments, which was chaired by Secretary Hughes. He introduced the discussion of this subject by reading a number of reports relating to chemical warfare. The first was prepared by the Committee's own technical subcommittee. This report noted, among other things, that "the kinds of gases and their effects on human beings can not be taken as a basis for limitation. . . . [T]hat the only limitation practicable is to wholly prohibit the use of gases against cities and other large bodies of noncombatants . . . but that there could be no limitation on their use against the armed forces of the enemy, ashore or afloat."[22] The second report, prepared by the Advisory Committee of the United States delegation, proposed that "chemical warfare, including the use of gases, whether toxic or nontoxic, should be prohibited by international agreement."[23] The next document to be presented by Mr. Hughes was a memorandum by the General Board of the Navy.[24] It asserted that the use of gas was "almost universally condemned" if it violated "the two principles in warfare, (1) that unnecessary suffering in the destruction of combatants should be avoided, [and] (2) that innocent noncombatants should not be destroyed." The Navy emphasized the following considerations:

> Certain gases, for example tear gas, could be used without violating the two principles above cited. Other gases will, no doubt, be invented which could be so employed; but there will be great difficulty in a clear definite demarcation between the lethal gases and those which produce unnecessary suffering as distinguished from those gases which simply disable temporarily.

The report accordingly closed with the declaration that "the General Board believes it to be sound policy to prohibit gas warfare in every form and against every objective, and so recommends."[25]

Having presented these reports to the Committee, Mr. Hughes made the following statement:

> [D]espite the conclusions reached by the subcommittee of this committee . . . the American delegation, in the light of the advice of its advisory committee and the concurrence in that advice of General Pershing . . . and of the specific recommendation of the General Board of the Navy, felt that it should present the recommendation that the use of asphyxiating or poison gas be absolutely prohibited.[26]

The resolution containing the text of what was to become Article 5 was introduced by Senator Root:

> Mr. Root said that the chairman[27] had asked him to prepare this resolution, pursuant to the recommendation of those military and naval authorities and advisory committees to which the American delegation was bound to pay the highest respect. There was an expression on this subject which presented the most extraordinary consensus of opinion that one could well find upon any international subject. He had drafted the resolution . . . in the language of the Treaty of Versailles which was subscribed to by the four of the five powers here and was appropriated and taken over by the United States and Germany in the treaty concluded between them on the 25th of August [1921]. . . .[28]

The resolution presented by Senator Root was adopted unanimously[29] and, although it sparked some general discussion, no attempt was made to explore the intended scope of the prohibition formulated in Article 5.

Legally the most significant aspect of the history of Article 5 of the Treaty of Washington is that not one of the delegations present made any attempt to exclude irritant chemicals from the prohibition of this clause. The legal significance of this omission derives from two interrelated facts: First, the reports Secretary Hughes presented to the Conference addressed themselves specifically to these weapons. Second, two of the three reports recommended a prohibition of all chemical weapons. The United States delegation relied expressly on these reports and specifically rejected, as too limited in scope, the recommendations of the technical subcommittee. It is therefore most unlikely that a government which believed that Article 5 did not outlaw all forms of chemical warfare would have failed to state its views to the Conference.[30]

(c) The Geneva Protocol. The Geneva Protocol was drafted at the Conference for the Supervision of the International Trade in Arms and Ammunition and in Implements of War, which was convened to consider the adoption of a comprehensive treaty relating to the international arms trade.[31] Noting that the draft treaty before the Conference did not contain a prohibition against the export of chemical weapons,[32] the United States delegation submitted two alternative texts deal-

·8

ing with this subject.[33] The first of these, after proclaiming that "the use in war of asphyxiating, poisonous or other gases, and all analogous liquids, materials or devices, has been justly condemned by the general opinion of the civilized world," would have bound the Contracting Parties "to prohibit the export from their territory of any such asphyxiating, poisonous or other gases and all analogous liquids, intended or designed for use in connection with operations of war." The other text provided that the Contracting Parties would "agree to control the traffic in poisonous gases by prohibiting the exportation of all asphyxiating, toxic or deleterious gases, and all analogous liquids, materials and devices manufactured and intended for use in warfare." When serious doubts were expressed at the Conference regarding the practicability of controlling the exportation of these chemicals since they had many peaceful industrial uses,[34] the United States proposed a separate instrument embodying the provisions of Article 5 of the Treaty of Washington.[35] This proposal was adopted[36] and explains why the chemical warfare prohibition of the Geneva Protocol came to be drafted in the language of Article 5.

No attempt was made at the Geneva Conference to discuss the scope of this prohibition and no reference to tear gas or other irritant chemicals appears in the records of the Conference. The only evidence pointing to an intention to exclude such agents is the statement of the United States delegate (Congressman Theodore E. Burton), who, in urging the adoption of a prohibition on the export of chemical weapons, expressed "the very earnest desire of the Government and people of the United States that some provision be inserted in this Convention relating to the use of asphyxiating, poisonous, and deleterious gases" and emphasized that a "prohibition of the exportation of these gases" would receive the "express approval" of President Calvin Coolidge.[37] No significance was attached to this statement in the Senate when it debated the advisability of ratification of the Protocol.[38] As a matter of fact, one of the arguments that was advanced in the Senate against the ratification of the Geneva Protocol was that it would prohibit the use in war of tear gases, even though they were harmless and had been adopted by "every intelligent police force in the United States." And while the floor manager of the treaty did not fail to emphasize immediately that the Geneva Protocol did not apply to the use of tear gas by the police, he apparently believed that it outlawed the use of this gas in an international conflict.[39]

2. *Post-1925 practice relating to the Geneva Protocol.*

(*a*) The Franco-British Interpretation of 1930. Until 1930 no government appears to have expressed the view that the Geneva Protocol did not outlaw all forms of chemical warfare. The issue was formally raised in November of that year in a memorandum by the British delegation to the League of Nations Preparatory Commission for the Disarmament Conference.[40] At the time this memorandum was submitted, the Preparatory Commission had under consideration a draft disarmament convention containing a provision relating to the "use in war of asphyxiating, poisonous or *similar* gases." The use of the word "similar" apparently prompted some delegations to inquire whether the departure from the formula of the English text of the Geneva Protocol was designed to restrict the prohibition on chemical warfare in the draft convention. Realizing that the different wording in the two official texts of the Geneva Protocol might support the argument that the Protocol did not, for example, outlaw tear gas and other irritant chemicals, the British delegation made the following statement:

> Basing itself on this English text [of the Geneva Protocol], the British Government have taken the view that the use in war of "other" gases, including lachrymatory gases, was prohibited. They also considered that the intention was to incorporate the same prohibition in the present Convention.

> From every point of view it is highly desirable that a uniform construction should prevail as to whether or not the use of lachrymatory gases is considered to be contrary to the Geneva Protocol. . . .[41]

The French delegation responded with the following statement:

> I. All the texts at present in force or proposed in regard to the prohibition of the use *in war* of asphyxiating, poisonous or similar gases are identical. In the French delegation's opinion, they apply to all gases employed with a view to toxic action on the human organism, whether the effects of such action are

more or less temporary irritation of certain mucous membranes or whether they cause serious or even fatal lesions.

II. The French military regulations, which refer to the undertaking not to use gas for warfare *(gaz de combat)* subject to reciprocity, classify such gases as suffocating, blistering, *irritant* and poisonous gases in general, and define irritant gases as those causing *tears,* sneezing, etc.

III. The French Government therefore considers that the use of lachrymatory gases is covered by the prohibition arising out of the Geneva Protocol. . . .
The fact that, for the maintenance of internal order, the police, when dealing with offenders against the law, sometimes use various appliances discharging irritant gases cannot, in the French delegation's opinion, be adduced in a discussion on this point, since the Protocol or Convention in question relates only to the use of poisonous or similar gases *in war.*[42]

At the time these declarations were made, the Geneva Protocol had been ratified by twenty-eight states, including France and Great Britain. Eighteen of these states were members of the Preparatory Commission.[43] Ten of them associated themselves expressly with the French and British interpretation, whereas the remaining six states did not respond to the British invitation for an expression of opinion.[44] And although a number of other states that subsequently ratified the Protocol also supported this interpretation, only the United States representative (Hugh Gibson) expressed doubts. Since the United States had not yet ratified the Geneva Protocol, he was careful not to offer an opinion on the prohibitory scope of that instrument. He addressed himself instead to the prohibition of chemical warfare that should be included in the draft convention. In that context, Mr. Gibson declared:

I think there would be considerable hesitation on the part of many Governments to bind themselves to refrain from the use in war, against an enemy, of agencies which they have adopted for peace-time use against their own population, agencies adopted on the ground that, while causing temporary inconvenience, they cause no real suffering or permanent disability, and are thereby more clearly humane than the use of weapons to which they were formerly obliged to resort to in times of emergency.[45]

Mr. Gibson concluded his statement with the proposal that

the Preparatory Commission not make a decision on the scope of the chemical warfare prohibition of the draft convention but that the states to be represented at the forthcoming Disarmament Conference "be requested to give this entire subject careful study and consideration, with a view to arriving at that Conference equipped with adequate knowledge of the problem in all its aspects."[46] This proposal was accepted by the Preparatory Conference.[47]

At the Disarmament Conference itself no attempt was made to interpret the Geneva Protocol. It is significant, however, that the special committee which studied the questions Mr. Gibson had raised recommended that

> . . . there should be included in qualitative disarmament the use, for the purpose of injuring an adversary, of all natural or synthetic noxious substances, whatever their state, whether solid, liquid or gaseous, whether toxic, asphyxiating, lachrymatory, irritant, vesicant, or capable in any way of producing harmful effects on the human or animal organism, whatever the method of their use.[48]

This recommendation was subsequently embodied in Article 48 of the draft convention, which provided that the prohibition of the use of chemical weapons applied "to the use, by any method whatsoever, for the purpose of injuring an adversary, of any natural or synthetic substance harmful to the human or animal organism, whether solid, liquid or gaseous, such as toxic, asphyxiating, lachrymatory, irritant or vesciant substances."[49] The United States found this provision acceptable.[50] The draft convention never entered into force for reasons unrelated to the scope of its prohibition of chemical and biological warfare.

To the extent that none of the states parties to the Protocol that were represented on the Preparatory Commission recorded their opposition to the British interpretation either during the meetings or within a reasonable period thereafter, they can be deemed to have assented thereto. The same is also true of the states parties to the Protocol that participated in the subsequent Disarmament Conference (all states which had up to that time ratified the Protocol were represented at the Conference), for they were on notice as to what had happened in the Preparatory Commission.[51]

(b) The post-1930 practice.[52] No state has at any time either before or after 1930 ratified or acceded to the Protocol with a reservation limiting the types of chemical weapons to which it applies. The fact that states acceding to the Protocol after 1930 did not enter a reservation excluding tear gas from the reach of the Protocol is particularly important because they had clearly been alerted to the interpretation of the treaty in that respect.

The use of tear gas and herbicides by the United States in Vietnam has provoked lengthy debates in the United Nations concerning the legality of these weapons. The United States has consistently asserted that the use of these weapons did not violate the Protocol.[53] Significantly, only one state party to the Protocol—Australia, which has troops in Vietnam—has associated itself in the United Nations with the United States view that the prohibition of the treaty applied neither to irritant chemicals nor to anti-plant chemicals.[54]

Great Britain has not associated itself with this view, but that government has declared that, although it still adhered to the position that "tear gases . . . are . . . prohibited under the Protocol," it considered that this prohibition did not extend to CS gas.[55]

On 16 December 1969, the United National General Assembly adopted a resolution[56] reciting its recognition "that the Geneva Protocol embodies the generally recognized rules of international law prohibiting the use in international armed conflicts of all biological and chemical methods of warfare, regardless of any technical developments. . . ." The resolution went on to declare

> as contrary to the generally recognized rules of international law, as embodied in the Protocol for the Prohibition of the Use in War of Asphyxiating, Poisonous or Other Gases, and of Bacteriological Methods of Warfare, signed at Geneva on 17 June 1925, the use in international armed conflicts of:
>
> (a) Any chemical agents of warfare—chemical substances, whether gaseous, liquid or solid—which might be employed because of their direct toxic effects on man, animals or plants. . . .

The resolution was adopted by eighty votes to three (the United States, Australia, and Portugal), with thirty-six absentions.[57] Although the vote cannot be regarded as a resounding affirmation of the proposition that irritant chemicals fall under the prohibition of the Protocol, the large number of states voting in favor of the resolution indicates that there is a very substantial amount of support for that view.

These few dissenting voices and thirty-six states whose silence supports neither one construction nor the other do not evidence any strong enthusiasm for a restrictive interpretation of the Protocol. And finally, legal niceties aside, what governments believe the Protocol to mean today probably counts for a good deal more than all of the other drafting history and subsequent practice put together.

3. *Conclusion.* The text of the prohibition of chemical warfare in the Geneva Protocol admits of both a broad and a restrictive interpretation of its intended scope. It is clear, however, that by their conduct and declarations in the past four decades the *parties* to the Protocol have demonstrated their understanding that this prohibition bars the use in war of all chemical agents having a direct toxic effect on man that might be used as anti-personnel weapons, including tear gas and other forms of irritant chemicals.

B. *Anti-Plant Chemicals*

The evidence is by no means as conclusive with regard to anti-plant chemicals. Since the Protocol speaks not only of "gases" but also of "all analogous liquids, materials or devices," its language permits the interpretation that anti-plant chemicals are included in the prohibition of the Protocol. Two arguments have been advanced against this interpretation. The first is that "the Protocol does not apply to herbicides, which involve the same chemicals and have the same effects as those used domestically in the United States, the Soviet Union and many other countries to control weeds and other unwanted vegetation."[58] This is an unpersuasive argument because, as the discussion relating to tear gas indicates, the fact that there are accepted peacetime uses for certain chemical agents does not make their use in war lawful. Moreover, the United States Department of Agriculture recently ordered one such supposedly harmless herbicide withdrawn from the market as a health hazard, and is investigating others. The use of this particular chemical agent, which was the defoliant most widely utilized in Vietnam, has in the meantime been suspended in that country.

The second argument is that the draftsmen of the Geneva Protocol could not possibly have intended to outlaw the use of herbicides because the military use of anti-plant chemicals was unknown at the time the treaty was negotiated.[59] From a legal point of view, it is of little importance that this information was lacking. Instead, the question that must be asked is what objectives was the Protocol intended to achieve? Herbicides would thus not come within its prohibition if it could be shown that the treaty was intended to outlaw the use in war only of anti-personnel chemical and biological weapons.

There is no evidence in the negotiating history of the Protocol to indicate that its draftsmen intended to *exclude* from its reach the use in war of plant-destroying chemical agents. There is, on the other hand, considerable evidence to justify the belief that the Protocol sought to outlaw chemical and biological warfare in general, irrespective of whether it was directed against human beings, animals, or plants.[60] The prohibition on biological warfare was clearly intended to have this comprehensive scope. The records of the Geneva Conference of 1925 indicate that the sponsor of this prohibition, the Polish representative, repeatedly warned that "great masses of men, animals and plants would be exterminated" unless biological warfare were outlawed.[61] The French representative in seconding the Polish proposal declared that, although "the extremely wide form of words" in which the prohibition of chemical warfare was expressed "should have been sufficient to cover bacteriological warfare," it was "not always a disadvantage to make an explicit reference, as the delegate for Poland had done."[62] It is therefore not unreasonable to assume that, had the combat uses of anti-plant chemicals been known, the Geneva Conference would have considered them to be within the prohibitory scope of the Protocol.

Note must, however, be taken of the fact that in 1930 the French government seemed to interpret the Protocol as forbidding the employment of chemical agents "with a view to toxic action on the human organism."[63] This is the only solid evidence from past history to support the doubts that some parties to the Protocol have recently expressed on its applicability to anti-plant chemicals.[64]

On balance, and taking the 1969 resolution of the General Assembly into account,[65] the case seems stronger for including anti-plant chemicals within the prohibition of the Protocol than for excluding them. It should be emphasized, however, that the evidence to support this interpretation is by no means as strong as is the evidence for including irritant chemicals within the chemicals prohibited by the agreement.

C. Bacteriological Warfare

The parties to the Geneva Protocol have agreed to a prohibition on "the use of bacteriological methods of warfare." There can be no doubt about this prohibition's embracing bacteriological methods of warfare against men, against animals, and against plants. The Polish delegate who proposed the addition of bacteriological methods of warfare to chemical ones in the Protocol drafted at the Geneva Conference of 1925 referred to the fact that "great masses of men, animals and plants would be exterminated" by bacteriological warfare.[66] In the ensuing years no doubt has been expressed about the comprehensiveness of the prohibition. The General Assembly resolution of 16 December 1969,[67] to which reference has previously been made, declared that the Protocol extends to any biological agents of warfare "which are intended to cause disease or death in man, animals or plants." This interpretation has also been espoused by the United States government.[68]

"War" and "Warfare" Within the Meaning of the Geneva Protocol

The Protocol contains two references to the types of conflict to which it applies. In the preamble, there is a reference to the fact that "the use in *war*" of gases has been condemned by the civilized world, and the operative portion of the Protocol declares that the parties agree to extend the prohibition of the use of chemical weapons to "bacteriological methods of *warfare*." The title of the Protocol describes the instrument as being "for the Prohibition of the Use in *War*" of chemical and bacteriological weapons.

"War" is obviously referred to in its material sense rather than in its formal sense as *declared* war. As described by Professor Julius Stone:

> International war is a relation of one or more governments to at least one other government, in which at least one of such governments no longer permits its relations with the other or others to be governed by the laws of peace. It is involved in this statement, as has been wittily observed, that while it takes two to make a quarrel, it takes only one government to make a war.[69]

And war is, as the above quotation indicates, international war—war between states. With the exception of a common article relating to civil conflicts, the four Geneva Conventions of 1949[70] apply to "all cases of declared war or of any other armed conflict which may arise between two or more of the High Contracting Parties, even if the state of war is not recognized by one of them."[71] The other principal treaty governing land warfare, the Regulations annexed to Convention No. IV of The Hague of 1907,[72] refers only to "war."

The understanding throughout the conventions dealing with the conduct of warfare is that they apply to war between states and do not apply to civil war, except insofar as may be expressly provided to the contrary.

General Assembly Resolution 2603 A (XXIV), 16 December 1969, refers to the prohibition not in "war" but in "international armed conflicts" of the agents defined in the Protocol. There appears to have been a certain reluctance in the First Committee and in the General Assembly about the use of this terminology,[73] which is, after all, consistent with the language of the Geneva Conventions of 1949. But it is to the Protocol and not to any General Assembly resolution that the United States would become a party, and in any event it would be patently out of keeping with the purposes of the Protocol to apply it in "war" but not in "international armed conflict"—as if any such distinction could be made for the purpose of the use of weapons in combat.

The Protocol thus does not apply of its own force to civil wars or to domestic disturbances. Difficulties can, of course, arise in connection with conflicts like the one in Vietnam which have some of the characteristics of international armed conflict and some of the characteristics of civil war. The characterization of such "mixed" conflicts is not a problem peculiar to the Geneva Protocol but cuts across all of the law of war.

If hostilities escalate to such a scale that one or more of the participants in civil conflict considers it appropriate to apply the Geneva Conventions of 1949 and The Hague Regulations of 1907, it would be difficult to maintain that the conflict is not "war" for the purposes of the Geneva Protocol of 1925. Consistency would seem to demand that the prohibitions of the Geneva Protocol become operative *pari passu* with the rest of the international law of war.

Does the use of gas against unruly prisoners of war constitute a use in "war"? It appears that it does, since prisoners of war rioting against the forces of the Detaining Power have in fact resumed hostilities against the Detaining Power and are engaged in "warfare" with it. It would be strange indeed if gas could not be used against enemy soldiers in combat but could be freely employed against them once they were taken prisoner. The very use of gas against prisoners awakens memories of the use of gas in the concentration camps of the Second World War.

The Existing Reservations by Other States

Thirty-nine states have entered reservations to the Geneva Protocol at the time of their accession or ratification.[74] With several exceptions, one here relevant and the others not, they fall into two standard forms, the language employed by various countries in each form of reservation being virtually identical.[75] The reservations of Great Britain will be taken as typical of both forms.

The first reservation provides that:

> The said protocol shall be binding on his Britannic Majesty only with respect to the Powers and States which have signed and ratified it or which have acceded to it permanently.

The purpose of this reservation was to make it altogether clear that the Protocol did not constitute a unilateral renunciation of the use of chemical and bacteriological weapons against all countries, whether or not parties to the Protocol. The Protocol thus operates on the principle of reciprocity of obligation. This mutuality of obligation is generally true of treaties on the conduct of warfare, and in The Hague Regulations[76] and in the Geneva Conventions of 1949[77] the principle is spelled out expressly. The reservations undoubtedly arise out of a fear that an adverse inference might be occasioned by the absence of similar unambiguous language of reciprocity in the Protocol. There is no reason to suppose that the draftsmen of the Protocol desired to depart from the usual principle of mutuality of obligation in treaties, but the differing formulation of the treaties on the conduct of warfare is troublesome.

If mutuality of obligation is required under the Protocol, whether according to its original terms or as modified by the reservations in this form, then a state party to the Protocol may employ chemical and bacteriological weapons against a non-party. If the Protocol is construed not to import any mutuality of obligation but to constitute a unilateral renunciation of the use of these methods of warfare by each party, then some protection is independently afforded to a party by the second reservation, which liberates a state from its obligation if there is in fact noncompliance with the treaty by an enemy state.

The fact that nineteen states have entered this reservation calling for reciprocity of obligation weakens the case for saying that this reciprocity is already implicit in the text of the Protocol. Prudence might therefore dictate that the United States reserve on the same basis as these states, which include five imporant members of NATO, the Soviet Union, and a number of its allies.

Two variants on this form of reservation call for comment. The British reservation, unlike some of the others, states that that country will be bound only to those states which have ratified or acceded to the Protocol "permanently." The use of this word excludes reciprocity with respect to a state that has become a party to the Protocol for a term of years or has given notice of its denunciation of the treaty but is still bound by it or in any other way has indicated that its intention is not to be permanently bound. This word appears to reflect an excess of caution, and the British example is not necessarily to be emulated.

The People's Republic of China has bound itself to apply the Protocol "subject to reciprocity on the part of all other contracting and acceding Powers." It is not clear whether this refers merely to factual mutuality in the performance of the treaty or extends also to mutuality of legal obligation.

The second standard form of reservation is, again in the language of the British reservation:

> The said protocol shall cease to be binding on His Britannic Majesty with respect to any enemy Power the armed forces of which or the armed forces allied with which fail to respect the interdictions which form the subject of this protocol.

Some of the reservations of this form (for example that of Canada) speak of "allies *de jure* or *de facto*."

In the strict sense, an "ally" is a state allied under a treaty of alliance. An "ally *de jure*" is to be understood in this sense. But allies may also simply be states that fight together without being linked by any treaty of alliance. They are "allies *de facto*." The more precise "allies *de jure* or *de facto*" probably does not differ in substance from the allied armed forces referred to in the British reservation.

Account must be taken of the fact that the expression "armed forces allied with which" could extend to forces, such as guerrillas and resistance movements, that do not depend on a particular state but do fight alongside an enemy power. Thus, the use of gas by a guerrilla force allied with an enemy state but not necessarily under its control would justify the use of gas against the armed forces of that enemy state.

The effect of the reservation is as follows: States A and B are allied in war against State C, which has entered the above reservation.[78] The armed forces of State B use gas against the forces of State C. State C, by the terms of its reservation, is no longer obliged to apply the Protocol as regards the forces of State A. The reservation apparently limits the obligation of State C whether or not States A and B have entered similar reservations. At the extreme, the reservation could apply to a more complex situation: States A and B are again allied in war against State C, which has reserved. State B is simultaneously engaged in war against State D. If State B uses even a whiff of gas against the forces of State D, under the terms of the reservation State C is freed of its obligation under the Protocol as regards both States A and B.

This reservation clearly goes beyond what would be permitted under customary international law in the absence of the reservation. Put briefly, in the language of the Vienna Convention on the Law of Treaties, "a party specially affected by the [material] breach [of a multilateral treaty by one of the parties to the treaty] [is entitled] to invoke it as a ground for suspending the operation of the treaty in whole or in part in the relations between itself and the defaulting state."[79] A party is also entitled, under the Vienna Convention, to suspend operation of the treaty in the same way if the material breach by one party "radically changes the position of every party with respect to the further performance of its obligations under the treaty."[80] This provision was directed toward treaties, such as disarmament treaties, where a breach by one party "tends to undermine the whole régime of the treaty."[81] However, the foregoing stipulations have no application to "provisions relating to the protection of the human person contained in treaties of a humanitarian character."[82]

First, a failure "to respect the interdictions" of the Protocol within the meaning of the reservation does not necessarily constitute a "material breach" of the Protocol, so that the circumstances releasing a state from its obligations under the reservation go well beyond what is permitted under international law. Second, it is only a state "specially affected" which is entitled not to perform, and the violation of the Protocol by an ally of an enemy of that state would not necessarily "specially affect" it. Third, the provision relating to a breach which radically changes the position of every party is directed particularly to disarmament treaties, which the Protocol is not. Fourth, the Protocol must probably be looked upon as a humanitarian treaty, like the Geneva Conventions of 1949, to which these provisions regarding the termination or suspension of the operation of a treaty as a consequence of its breach do not apply.

Nor can the terms of the reservation be construed as merely confirming a power to engage in reprisals, since these are temporary departures from the law justified by and directed toward another state's antecedent violation of the law and designed to coerce that state into renewed compliance with the law. The law imposes requirements of a demand for compliance, lack of other alternatives, and proportionality, none of which are implicit in the reservation.[83] Moreover, the Geneva Civilians Convention of 1949 forbids reprisals against civilians[84] and the Prisoners of War Convention against prisoners of war.[85] It would be difficult to avoid affecting these two categories of persons if chemical or bacteriological methods of warfare were to be employed.

In its relations with states, such as the Soviet Union, that have entered this reservation, the United States would be entitled to avail itself of the reservation on a basis of reciprocity.[86] Thus, if the United States were to engage in war with the Soviet Union and an ally of the Soviet Union were to employ gas, the United States would be entitled to terminate performance under the treaty.

The danger of the second form of reservation is that seemingly any violation of the Protocol could constitute a failure "to respect the interdictions" of the Protocol and would release the aggrieved state from all of its obligations under the Protocol vis-à-vis the offending state and its allies. In the absence of verification of which state engaged in "first use," it would be impossible to determine whether a state unlawfully initiated use of chemical weapons or was merely responding to an antecedent violation of the Protocol. The reservation offers an easy way for combatants to slip into the forbidden forms of warfare.

On the other hand, a reservation to this effect by the United States would assure it of the same measure of protection in the event of a breach of the Protocol by an enemy that is now enjoyed by Great Britain, a number of other NATO partners, and the Soviet Union, not only in relation to those states but to others as well. The reservation also has the merit of taking account of the fact that in these days international conflicts are usually fought by coalitions and that what is done by the ally of an enemy state may have as profound an impact upon a belligerent state as if it had been the work of the enemy state itself. The reservation simply recognizes that there are two *sides* in a conflict and that what is done by a participant on one side has an impact on all states arrayed on the other side.

Possible Legal Positions That Might Be Taken On Irritant Chemicals and Anti-Plant Chemicals

There is a variety of legal positions that the United States might take with respect to irritant gases and anti-plant chemicals if it ratifies the Geneva Protocol. A decision on what line to take will require that the United States government has made up its mind on the interpretation to be attached to the Protocol by that country and on the degree of freedom that that country desires to retain. Different treatment might be given to irritant chemicals and anti-plant chemicals.

The range of possibilities seems to be as follows:

1. *Acceptance of the view that irritant gases and/or anti-plant chemicals fall within the scope of the Geneva Protocol.* In view of the fact that the United States appears hitherto to have inclined to the view that irritant gases and anti-plant chemicals are not prohibited by the Protocol, selection of this option might well be accompanied by a statement, which might or might not form part of the instrument of ratification, whereby the United States would indicate its understanding about the scope of the Protocol. The United States might, for

example, state that it is willing to accept the obligation not to use these two forms of chemical weapons and note the concurrence of the eighty members of the United Nations that voted for this interpretation in the General Assembly resolution of 1969. Such a statement would have the beneficial effect of bringing about greater harmonization in the interpretation of the Protocol and might *encourager les autres*. On the other hand, by putting its understanding on record as to either or both forms of chemical, the United States would be committing itself to that interpretation. It would thus have less freedom of action than other states that have not expressed themselves and may jump one way or the other when a decision must be made about the applicability of the Protocol to these types of chemicals.

2. *Acceptance of the view that irritant gases and/or anti-plant chemicals fall within the scope of the Geneva Protocol, accompanied by the drawing up of a protocol whereby the United States and others might indicate their shared understanding of the Geneva Protocol.* This option would differ from the foregoing in that the United States would take the initiative in drawing up an instrument whereby it and other states would indicate their understanding of the scope of the Geneva Protocol. It would be open to countries to become parties to the protocol to the Geneva Protocol and thereby put themselves on record as to their interpretation of the Protocol. While the existence of that protocol might be a stimulus to other nations to declare themselves, it might on the other hand divide the parties to the Protocol into two camps—those willing to exclude the use of anti-plant chemicals or irritant chemicals and those nations which, by deliberately refusing to become parties to the new instrument, would show that they reserved the right to use such weapons.

3. *Leaving open the question whether irritant chemicals and/or anti-plant chemicals are excluded by the Geneva Protocol, without taking any position on the matter.* Although this option is theoretically open, it would as a practical matter be extremely difficult to maintain silence on these issues. It is inevitable that questions would be asked in the Senate when the advice and consent of that body are sought and that other

governments would be curious about the position of the United States. And if the United States desired to continue to use such weapons, this strategy would not be an effective way of building support for the lawfulness of such conduct by that country. Options 4 and 5 would be more effective than silence.

4. *Indication by the United States that it understands the Geneva Protocol not to exclude the use of irritant chemicals and/or anti-plant chemicals without inclusion of any such statement in the instrument of ratification.* The United States could simply indicate that it understands the Protocol to permit the use of either irritant gases or anti-plant chemicals or of both types of chemical agents. This might be done through a statement by the President in submitting the Protocol to the Senate or by reading this understanding into the legislative history, as, for example, by an appropriate statement in the report of the Senate Foreign Relations Committee.[87] There could be some pressure within the Senate to move from this position to an outright reservation, but this embarrassment could be avoided if proper advance consultation were to be made.

The advantage of this posture is that the United States would thereby indicate it considers that it would have liberty of action to employ these weapons after ratifying the Protocol, without making itself the target of objections, as might follow from the employment of Option 5 or 6. Foreign states might not feel compelled to take issue with the United States, although understanding what its position is. In time other states might come to accept this interpretation of the Protocol. On the other hand, the United States would not be assured of freedom to use such weapons, in the face of a contrary interpretation attached to the Protocol by the other parties to the instrument. Only Option 6 could assure that degree of security. The United States would in any event have to face the risk that there might be a variety of differing interpretations by other states, to which it would simply add one more.

5. *A clear statement, conveyed in its instrument of ratification, that the United States adheres to the view that the Geneva Protocol does not cover irritant gases and/or anti-plant chemicals.* The United States could, at the time of rati-

fying the Geneva Protocol, declare in the instrument of ratification its understanding that certain weapons are excluded from the Protocol. The United States would not thereby be legally protected in the use of such weapons but might hope to persuade other states to agree that such weapons are not covered by the Protocol. If that could be accomplished, enough doubt could be raised about the meaning of the treaty that it would be difficult to maintain that the United States had committed any clear-cut violation of the treaty through the employment of these weapons.

There would be advantages and disadvantages in such a course of action.

It is true that "[a] party may make a declaration which indicates the meaning that it attaches to a provision of an agreement but which it does not regard as changing the legal effect of the provision."[88] The understanding may be looked upon as just "one man's opinion" possessing exactly the same relevance as any individual state's understanding of the agreement. But it would be open to other states to construe the understanding or declaration as an attempt by the United States to limit its obligations, and those states might choose to treat the understanding or declaration as a reservation.[89] The United States would thus remain at the mercy of other states. If they treat the statement as merely the understanding of the United States, the understanding is only one bit of evidence to be weighed in the balance; if they treat it as a reservation, the consequences alluded to below follow.

Such a course of action, like Option 4, would in all likelihood permit the United States to become a party to the Protocol without embarrassing objections and would buy the government time to try to persuade other states to change their views. Whether the United States would be able to accomplish this is conjectural, and it might be that that country and Great Britain would be faced with widespread objection to the exclusion of tear gas.

If the United States were to maintain that the Protocol does not cover irritant gases or anti-plant chemicals or both, whether in the instrument of ratification or otherwise, that course of action would promote diversity of interpretation of an instrument that should receive a uniform construction if it is to operate effectively. If an enemy state should construe the Protocol as prohibiting the use of tear gas and the United States should nevertheless use that weapon, the enemy state might then tax the United States with the first violation of the agreement and use other forms of chemical and bacteriological warfare under claim of right. It would be easy to cast off the restraints of the Protocol in an argument about how far it carries. Thus the continued use of tear gas by the United States could lead to retaliatory use of far more devastating chemicals by a state claiming that it is acting in full conformity with the law.

6. *A reservation that would have the effect of giving the United States full legal protection in the use of irritant gases and/or anti-plant chemicals.* On becoming a party to the Protocol, the United States could be legally secure in continuing to use irritant gases or anti-plant chemicals or both only by entering a reservation under which this country would seek to alter its obligation under the Protocol.

The problem about a reservation is that it is open to the other parties to the treaty either to accept or reject the reservation, since it constitutes a counter offer by the reserving state to the offer made by all of the other parties to the treaty in its original form. The Soviet Union and its allies have generally been in favor of allowing states freely to make reservations to treaties in the exercise of their sovereignty. However, while the war in Vietnam continues, and this soon after the General Assembly resolution of 1969, it is too much to expect that the Soviet Union would remain silent in the face of a reservation by the United States. And even if the Soviet Union were to raise no objection some other state might.

If a state objects that the reservation is "incompatible with the object and purposes of the treaty,"[90] either one of two consequences may follow:

a. The provisions of the treaty to which the reservation relates do not apply as between the two parties to the extent of the reservation, or

b. The treaty does not enter into force between the reserving and the objecting states, if that is the intention of the objecting state.[91]

The difficulty with the first possibility is that it may not be easy to establish exactly what "provisions" do not apply. If the provisions are those referring to "asphyxiating, poisonous or other gases," the deletion of these provisions in treaty relations between the United States and an objecting state would effectively emasculate the treaty. If only "other gases" are involved, to allow the deletion of this much of the Protocol would amount to an acceptance of a reservation as to irritant gases. But the possibility would still exist that an objecting state would assert that it was better (and perhaps conducive to the withdrawal of a reservation by the United States) if that state refused to accept the reservation and were to deny treaty relations with the United States. One of the risks of a reservation is therefore the possibility that the United States would not be bound as to an objecting state. Faced with that situation, it would of course be open to the United States, with the consent of the Senate, to withdraw the reservation and assume full treaty relations with the objecting state, if that course of action were on balance to be considered desirable.

Acceptance of a reservation, either expressly or through silence, brings the treaty into force between the reserving and accepting states subject to the reservation, which can be relied upon by the accepting state as well, on a basis of reciprocity.

To sum up, the other parties to the Protocol hold the whip hand, for each may, in its discretion, accept a United States reservation, regard the provision to which the reservation applies as not being in force, or reject treaty relations under the Protocol altogether.

7. *Securing an authoritative interpretation of the Geneva Protocol through an advisory opinion of the International Court of Justice.* Elucidation of the text of the Protocol could come from the International Court of Justice. The most feasible way of securing that clarification would be through an advisory opinion of the International Court requested by the Security Council or the General Assembly or a specialized agency of the United Nations pursuant to Article 96 of the United Nations Charter. The decision whether to seek an

advisory opinion would naturally rest with those bodies. The United States government might wish to take the initiative in proposing such action to supplement the measures contemplated under Options 1 through 5. The United States would thereby have a means to press its own understanding of the Protocol and then to yield gracefully if the decision were to go against it.

The United States might go further. It could state its understanding of the meaning of the Protocol but agree that it would be bound by any advisory opinion that might be rendered by the Court. It is reasonable to suppose that that decision would not bear out the United States contention that irritant chemicals and anti-plant chemicals fall outside the scope of the Protocol.

The United States would have to reckon with the possibility that the General Assembly or the Security Council might not be willing to seek an advisory opinion. In the case of the Security Council, the casting of the double veto could preclude resort to the Court. The first veto would be cast on the characterization of the matter as substantive or procedural. The exercise of the veto would then in all likelihood dictate that the question be treated as a substantive one, which would be subject to a second exercise of the veto. Exactly how the matter would be handled would depend to a large measure on the views of the person who happened to be President of the Security Council at that time.

The case for the desirability and the acceptability of resort to the International Court is not as clear as might appear on first impression. Several recent decisions by the Court—notably that in the *South West Africa* cases[92]—have been received with a marked lack of enthusiasm. We are in a period of somewhat diminished confidence in the Court, which might make it difficult to persuade states to take the matter to that body.

From the point of view of the United States, the possibility would have to be faced that a proposed submission to the Court could be used as the occasion for propaganda against the United States. If the request for an advisory opinion were to originate in the General Assembly (which would be the logical way), there would be no way to prevent states from making an issue of the practices of the United States in the Vietnam conflict, both as to chemical and bacteriological warfare and as to the conduct of that war in general. The conduct of the United States would also be material in the arguments before the Court, for the case for the prohibition of tear gas and defoliants under the Protocol might be based on the harm in fact caused by these weapons.

And, finally, an advisory opinion would not be binding on the General Assembly or other organ or specialized agency requesting it. If the Court were to come down on the side of interpreting the Protocol to prohibit anti-plant chemicals and irritant gases, there is little likelihood that the General Assembly would object to that conclusion. Since the United States has taken a strong line in the past on the General Assembly's giving effect to the advisory opinions of the Court, it would be difficult for the United States to do other than comply with the decision of the Court, whatever may be the views of the United States government on the legal effect of resolutions of the General Assembly. But if the Court were to take a position that did not find favor in the eyes of a majority of the members of the General Assembly—as, for example, by agreeing that tear gas is outside the scope of the Protocol —that organ is not required to follow the Court. Although the Court's views have generally been accepted in the past, they do not have to be. The General Assembly could attempt to impose its own interpretation of the Protocol on the United States through an overwhelming vote in that body.

Although these hazards would have to be weighed in the balance, an authoritative interpretation of the Protocol by the International Court might provide the United States with a reasonable and acceptable way to stop the use of chemicals found by the Court to be within the prohibition of the Protocol.

8. *Other modes of clearing up disagreement about the Geneva Protocol.* Even though no advisory opinion of the International Court were to be sought, the possibility exists that the adoption of Option 4 or 5 might lead a state to bring an action against the United States within the contentious jurisdiction of the Court. In that event, the United States

would be forced to assert the defense of the Connally Reservation, whereby the United States excludes from its acceptance of the compulsory jurisdiction of the Court "matters which are essentially within the domestic jurisdiction of the United States of America as determined by the United States of America."[93] The United States would probably be protected by its assertion that the use of irritant chemicals and anti-plant chemicals in warfare is within the domestic jurisdiction of the United States as determined by that country. That defense could be waived but probably only with the consent of the Senate.

The parties to the Protocol could seek to clear up their differences through negotiation. These discussions could in time lead to the adoption of a formal instrument interpreting the agreement, as contemplated in Option 2.

REFERENCES

1. For the official French and English texts of the Geneva Protocol, see League of Nations Treaty Series 94 (1929): 65.

2. These statistics have been supplied by the United States Department of State and include states that are bound by the Protocol by virtue of its ratification by governments which they succeeded.

3. The Geneva Protocol was drafted at the Conference on International Trade in Arms, which was convened by the League of Nations and met in Geneva from 4 May through 17 June 1925. For the official records of this conference, see League of Nations, *Proceedings of the Conference for the Supervision of the International Trade in Arms and Ammunition and in Implements of War (1925)*, hereinafter cited as *1925 Geneva Conference Proceedings.*

4. The Geneva Protocol was transmitted to the United States Senate for its advice and consent on 12 January 1926. It was not put to a vote because the unexpected opposition that had developed to it prompted the Chairman of the Foreign Relations Committee (Senator William Borah) to have the Protocol referred back to his Committee. This was done on 13 December 1926. See U.S., *Congressional Record,* Vol. 68 (1927), p. 368. It was not reported out of that Committee again and was among a number of treaties that were withdrawn by President Harry S. Truman in 1947 "with a view to placing the treaty calendar on a current basis." U.S. Dept. of State *Bulletin,* Vol. 16 (1947), p. 726.

5. Convention on the Law of Treaties, opened for signature at Vienna, 23 May 1969, art. 31, para. 1. United Nations Doc. A/CONF. 39/27, 23 May 1969.

6. Art. 31, para. 3(b).

7. Art. 32 describes recourse to the *travaux préparatoires* as "supplementary means of interpretation."

8. The customary international law on this subject is not altogether free from doubt. The authorities for the most part take the view that customary international law prohibits chemical warfare, at least insofar as lethal chemicals are concerned. See, for example, H. Meyrowitz, *Les Armes biologiques et le droit international* (Paris: Pedone, 1968); Robert W. Tucker, *The Law of War and Neutrality at Sea,* U.S. Naval War College, International Law Studies, Vol. 50 (Washington: U.S. Govt. Printing Office, 1957), p. 52; I. Brownlie, "Legal Aspects of CBW," in Steven Rose, ed., *CBW: Chemical and Biological Warfare* (Boston: Beacon Press, 1969), pp. 148–149; and W. V. O'Brien, "Biological/Chemical Warfare and the International Law of War," *Georgetown Law Journal,* Vol. 51 (1962), p. 36. United States Department of the Army, *The Law of Land Warfare,* Field Manual 27-10, (1956), para. 38, takes no position on the state of customary international

law and contents itself with a recital that the United States "is not a party to any treaty, now in force, that prohibits or restricts the use in warfare of toxic or nontoxic gases. . . ."

There is a split of opinion on whether customary international law also forbids the use of irritant chemicals and anti-plant chemicals. United Nations General Assembly Res. 2603 A, adopted on 16 December 1969, declared "as contrary to the generally recognized rules of international law, as embodied in the [Geneva] Protocol . . . the use in international armed conflicts of: (a) Any chemical agents of warfare—chemical substances, whether gaseous, liquid or solid—which might be employed because of their direct toxic effects on man, animals or plants." But Resolution 2603 A was adopted by 80 votes to 3, with 36 abstentions, and the dissenting and abstaining states included most of the members of NATO and a number of other important military powers, many of them parties to the Protocol. See UN Doc. A/PV.1836, 16 Dec. 1969, pp. 16, 17.

9. The Geneva Protocol stipulates that the "French and English texts are both authentic."

10. Those who espouse this argument generally overlook the fact that the phrase "gaz toxiques" includes, as a matter of French usage, all chemical weapons that are employed for their toxic effect on living organisms. It thus applies to such irritant chemicals as tear gas. See Meyrowitz, op. cit., pp. 38–39; and *Statement of the French Delegation Submitted to the Preparatory Commission for the Disarmament Conference* (1930), para. I. See pp. 10–11. Moreover, chemical agents of warfare are generally defined as chemical substances, whether gaseous, liquid, or solid, which are employed because of their *direct toxic* effect on man, animals, and plants. See, for example, *Chemical and Bacteriological (Biological) Weapons and the Effects of their Possible Use,* UN Pub. Sales No. E.69.I.24 (1969). This excludes certain chemicals now employed in warfare, such as high explosives, smoke, and incendiary substances (napalm, magnesium, white phosphorus, etc.), which exert their primary effects through physical force, fire, air-deprivation, or reduced visibility.

11. See G. Bunn, "Banning Poison Gas and Germ Warfare: Should the United States Agree?" *Wisconsin Law Review* (1969), pp. 396–397.

12. Statement by the U.S. Representative (Nabrit) to the United Nations General Assembly, 5 December 1966, reprinted in U.S., Arms Control and Disarmament Agency, *Documents on Disarmament, 1966*, p. 801.

13. For an analysis of the history of this language, see Bunn, "Banning Poison Gas and Germ Warfare," op. cit., pp. 397–402; and A. B. Overweg, *Die chemische Waffe und das Völkerrecht* (Berlin: E.S. Mittler, 1937), pp. 64–89.

14. See A. A. Fries and C. J. West, *Chemical Warfare* (New York: McGraw-Hill, 1921), pp. 15–16.

15. Treaty of Peace between the Principal Allied and Associated Powers and Germany, signed at Versailles, 28 June 1919, *Great Britain Treaty Series,* 1919, no. 4.

16. An early English-language draft of a provision that subsequently became Article 171 employed the phrase "or similar gases," but this wording was changed to "or other gases" in the drafting committee. Bunn asserts that there is no indication that any change in meaning was intended when "other" was substituted for "similar." Bunn, "Banning Poison Gas and Germ Warfare," op. cit., p. 398. He uses this to support a restrictive interpretation of "other." However, the broad sense in which the original term "similar" was used is clear when one examines the full text of the original provision. It read: "Production or use of asphyxiating, poisonous or similar gases, any liquid, any material and any similar device *capable of use in war* are [sic] forbidden." See U.S. Dept. of State, "The Paris Peace Conference 1919," *Foreign Relations of the United States,* Vol. 4 (Washington, D.C.: U.S. Govt. Printing Office, 1943), p. 232 (emphasis added).

17. U.S., Congress, Senate, *Conference on the Limitation of Armament* (1922), p. 888.

18. U.S., *Congressional Record,* Vol. 62 (1922), pp. 4723–4730.

19. Ibid., p. 4729.

20. U.S., Congress, Senate, *Conference on the Limitation of Armament* (1922).

21. Ibid., pp. 384–395.

22. Ibid., pp. 384–385.

23. Ibid., p. 386.

24. Ibid., pp. 386–387.

25. Ibid., p. 387.

26. Ibid., pp. 387–388.

27. Mr. Hughes.

28. *Conference on the Limitation of Armament,* op. cit., p. 388.

29. Ibid., p. 394.

30. It is true, of course, that Secretary Hughes spoke at one point only of an absolute prohibition of "the use of asphyxiating or poison gas." But this does not detract from the point being made in the text. If the United States Government had in fact intended to limit the scope of Article 5 to "the use of asphyxiating or poison gas," prudence would have dictated an unequivocal statement to that effect. And this precisely because the United States delegation had expressly associated itself with the views of its advisory committee and the General Board of the Navy.

31. See note 3 above.

32. *1925 Geneva Conference Proceedings,* p. 155.

33. Ibid., p. 779.
34. See, for example, ibid., pp. 528–535, 306–308.
35. Ibid., p. 310.
36. Ibid., p. 316.
37. Ibid., p. 155.
38. U.S., *Congressional Record,* Vol. 68 (1927), pp. 141–154, 226–229, 363–368.
39. Thus, after Senator Borah, the floor manager of the treaty, assured Senator James Reed that the Geneva Protocol did not apply to the use of tear gas by police, the latter replied that it outlawed the use of that gas in an international conflict and then asked, "Would it not be more merciful, assuming that we were at war with some Central American country, to win our battles by the temporary disabling of our enemies than to blow them all over their cactus plants . . . ?" Senator Borah answered this question by asking, "if you put them to sleep for a limited period, unless you took them prisoners and held them, they would be ready for battle the next day, would they not?" Ibid., p. 150.
40. This memorandum is reproduced in League of Nations, *Documents of the Preparatory Commission for the Disarmament Conference* (Series X); Minutes of the Sixth Session (Second Part, 1931), p. 311.
41. Ibid.
42. Ibid. (emphasis in the original).
43. The remaining 10 states, although not represented on the Preparatory Commission, were members of the League of Nations, under whose auspices the Commission was operating.
44. See League of Nations, *Documents of the Preparatory Commission,* op. cit., pp. 311–314.
45. Ibid., p. 312.
46. Ibid.
47. Ibid., p. 113. See also League of Nations, *Report of the Preparatory Commission for the Disarmament Conference,* U.S. Dept. of State Conference Series, no. 7, 1931, p. 45.
48. League of Nations, *Conference for the Reduction and Limitation of Armaments: Conference Documents,* Vol. 1 (1932), p. 214.
49. League of Nations, *Conference for the Reduction and Limitation of Armaments: Conference Documents,* Vol. 2 (1935), p. 488.
50. Minutes of the General Commission (December 14, 1932–June 29, 1933), League of Nations, *Records of the Conference for the Reduction and Limitation of Armaments* (Series B), Vol. 2 (1933) p. 569; and Letter, Secretary of State Hull to Chairman of American Delegation, 23 March 1933, *Foreign Relations of the United States,* 1933, Vol. 1 (1950), p. 75.
51. It must be remembered that the interpretation of the Protocol was advanced by France and Great Britain, the leading military powers

that had ratified the Protocol, and was supported in the Preparatory Commission by Italy, Spain, and the Soviet Union, among others.

52. For a very thorough treatment of the post-1930 practice, see Stockholm International Peace Research Institute, *The Problem of Chemical and Biological Warfare* (Provisional ed., 1970), Part III: CBW at the League of Nations and the United Nations, 1920–1969, pp. 64–277.

53. See, for example, United National General Assembly Official Records (GAOR): 21st Sess., 1966, 1st Cmtee., 1452nd Mtg., 14 Nov. 1966, paras. 38–41, and UN Doc. A/C.1/PV.1717, 10 Dec. 1969, p. 18. Various other official U.S. statements on this question can be found in the annual *Documents on Disarmament,* of the United States Arms Control and Disarmament Agency.

54. An Australian representative in the General Assembly stated: "It is the view of the Australian Government that the use of non-lethal substances such as riot control agents, herbicides and defoliants does not contravene the Geneva Protocol nor customary international law." UN Doc. A/C.1/PV.1716, 9 Dec. 1969, p. 87.

55. This position was justified by Michael Stewart, Secretary of State for Foreign and Commonwealth Affairs, in reliance on a 1930 Parliamentary statement in which the British government expressed the view that smoke screens, unlike tear gas, were not prohibited by the Protocol. The explanation given by Mr. Stewart reads as follows: "[M]odern technology has developed CS smoke which, unlike the tear gases available in 1930, is considered to be not significantly harmful to man in other than wholly exceptional circumstances; and we regard CS and other such gases accordingly as being outside the scope of the Geneva Protocol. CS is in fact less toxic than the screening smokes which the 1930 statement specifically excluded." Great Britain, *Parliamentary Debates* (Commons), Vol. 795, no. 50, p. 18 (Written Answers to Questions) (1970).
Neither the language of the Geneva Protocol nor previous statements by the British government afford any basis for a distinction between more toxic tear gases prohibited by the Protocol and less toxic gases not so prohibited. Besides, the tear gases that were used in the First World War were also not deemed to be harmful to man. See Fries and West, *Chemical Warfare,* op. cit., p. 15. The British view regarding CS gas would thus seem to be untenable.

56. General Assembly Res. 2603 A (XXIV), 16 Dec. 1969.

57. UN Doc. A/PV.1836, 16 Dec. 1969, p. 16.

58. Statement by the U.S. Representative (Nabrit) to the United Nations General Assembly, 5 Dec. 1966, *Documents on Disarmament, 1966,* op. cit., p. 801.

59. Statement of U.S. Representative (Leonard) in the First Committee. See UN Doc. A/C.1/PV.1717, 10 Dec. 1969, p. 21.

60. In 1924 the Temporary Mixed Commission for the Reduction of Armaments, whose report served as a preparatory document for the 1925 Geneva Conference, examined the effect of gas and biological agents on plants. It concluded that only the latter could be used against plants. League of Nations, *Report of the Temporary Mixed Commission for the Reduction of Armaments* (1924), p. 28. This conclusion, besides explaining why anti-plant chemicals were not discussed at the Geneva Conference, indicates that the draftsmen of the Protocol cannot be assumed to have wished to limit its scope to anti-personnel chemicals.

61. *1925 Geneva Conference Proceedings,* op. cit., p. 340.

62. Ibid., p. 341.

63. For the full text of the French statement, see pp. 10–11.

64. See, for example, statements of the French and Dutch governments, United Nations GAOR: 21st Sess., 1st Cmtte., 1461st Mtg., 23 Nov. 1966, paras. 31–37.

65. General Assembly Res. 2603 A (XXIV), 16 Dec. 1969.

66. *1925 Geneva Conference Proceedings,* op. cit., p. 340.

67. General Assembly Res. 2603 A (XXIV), 16 Dec. 1969.

68. Statement by T. R. Pickering, Deputy Director, Bureau of Politico-Military Affairs, Department of State, in U.S. Congress, House, Committee on Foreign Affairs, Subcommittee on National Security Policy and Scientific Developments, *Chemical-Biological Warfare: U.S. Policies and International Effects* (Washington, D.C.: U.S. Govt. Printing Office, 1970), pp. 179–180.

69. *Legal Controls of International Conflict* (New York: Rinehart, 1954), pp. 304–305; see also Majorie Whiteman, *Digest of International Law,* Vol. 10 (1968), pp. 1–26.

70. Signed 12 August 1949. United States Treaties and Other International Agreements (U.S.T.), Vol. 6, no. 3114; Treaties and Other International Acts Series (T.I.A.S.), Nos. 3362–3365. Common article 3 applies to "armed conflict not of an international character."

71. Common article 2 supra.

72. 36 Stat. (U.S. Statutes at Large) 2277, Treaty Series (T.S.), No. 539.

73. See, for example, the remarks of the delegates of Canada and Australia in the First Committee, UN Doc. A/C.1/PV.1716, 9 Dec. 1969.

74. The reservations are reproduced in Department of State, Division of Language Services, LS No. 12575, 3 Oct. 1967 [semble 1969], annexed to Statement by T. R. Pickering, Deputy Director, Bureau of Politico-Military Affairs, Department of State, before the Subcommittee on National Security Policy and Scientific Developments of the House Foreign Affairs Committee, 11 Dec. 1969 (mimeo). This appears to be a more recent and authoritative list than that in G. Bunn, "Banning Poison Gas and Germ Warfare," op. cit.

75. Account being taken, of course, of the different languages in which the reservations were framed.
76. Article 2 of Convention No. IV of The Hague of 1907, 36 Stat. 2277, T.S. No. 539, provides that "the provisions contained in the Regulations referred to in Article 1, as well as in the present Convention, do not apply except between Contracting Powers, and then only if all the belligerents are parties to the Convention."
77. Common article 2 provides that the Conventions apply "to all cases of declared war or of any other armed conflict which may arise between two or more of the High Contracting Parties." Supra note 70.
78. Without, it is assumed, objection by any other party to the Protocol.
79. Convention on the Law of Treaties, opened for signature at Vienna, 23 May 1969, art. 60, para. 2 (b), UN Doc. A/CONF.39/27, 23 May 1969, hereinafter referred to as the Vienna Convention. The Convention is not yet in force and is not retroactive, but it is nevertheless a highly authoritative guide to the interpretation of all treaties.
80. Ibid., art. 60, para. 2 (c).
81. Report of the International Law Commission on the work of its eighteenth session (1966), *Yearbook of the International Law Commission,* Vol. 2, p. 255, UN Doc. A/CN.4/SER.A/1966/ Add. 1 (1967).
82. Vienna Convention, art. 60, para. 5.
83. L. I. Oppenheim, *International Law,* 7th ed., ed. H. Lauterpacht, Vol. 2: *Disputes, War and Neutrality* (New York: Longmans, Green, 1952), pp. 136–144, 561–565.
84. Article 33, U.S.T., Vol. 6, p. 3516; T.I.A.S., no. 3365.
85. Article 13, U.S.T., Vol. 6, p. 3316; T.I.A.S., no. 3364.
86. Vienna Convention, art. 21, para. 1(b).
87. Testimony before the Senate Foreign Relations Committee was used to record various understandings by the United States of the meaning of the Treaty on Non-Proliferation of Nuclear Weapons. See U.S. Congress, Senate, Committee on Foreign Relations, *The Treaty on the Non-Proliferation of Nuclear Weapons: Hearings,* 90th Cong., 2d Sess., 1968, pp. 5–6.
88. American Law Institute, *Restatement (Second) of the Foreign Relations Law of the United States* (St. Paul, Minn.: American Law Institute Pub., 1965), § 124, comment c.
89. Ibid.; Charles Cheney Hyde, *International Law Chiefly as Interpreted and Applied by the United States,* Vol. 2 (2d. rev. ed., Boston: Little, Brown, 1945), p. 1436.
90. Vienna Convention, art. 19.
91. Vienna Convention, art. 20, para. 4(b), and art. 21, para. 3.
92. International Court of Justice, South West Africa Case, *Reports of Judgments, Advisory Opinions and Orders, 1966.*
93. Declaration signed by the President, Aug. 14, 1946, 61 Stat. 1218, T.I.A.S., no. 1598.

THE USE OF HERBICIDES IN WAR:
A POLITICAL/MILITARY ANALYSIS

by David E. Brown

"Anti-plant agents," according to a current United States Army training manual, are "chemical agents which possess a high offensive potential for destroying or seriously limiting the production of food and defoliating vegetation." The manual goes on to say further that

> these compounds include herbicides that kill or inhibit the growth of plants; plant growth regulators that either regulate or inhibit plant growth, sometimes causing plant death; dessicants that dry up plant foliage. . . . Military applications for anti-plant agents are based on denying the enemy food and concealment.[1]

United States armed forces have developed and refined herbicide delivery systems for use in the Vietnam conflict. Elaborate guidelines govern the delivery of herbicides, generally by specially-equipped cargo aircraft, onto selected targets. Defoliation—the reduction of undesired vegetation—has been the primary use of herbicides in Vietnam. They have also been used to a more limited extent for crop destruction.

Herbicides are a relatively recent addition to the U.S. arsenal.[2] Until about 1960, herbicide weapons were thought of as an intriguing technological possibility of dubious virtue. Our growing involvement in the Vietnam war created imperatives that stimulated field testing. Once the weapon was available additional uses were found for it. Since herbicides were initially in plentiful supply, the weapon was used with ever greater intensity. From limited testing in 1961-1962, the U.S. moved to the reduction of foliage along roads and waterways (1963), destruction of crops "grown by or for the enemy" (1964), and then to the spraying of large tracts of swamp and forest in 1965-1966. By 1967-1968, more than 2,000 square miles per year were subject to herbicide attack, an annual expenditure of some five million gallons of chemical herbicide. This was reportedly insufficient volume to meet all approved requests from field commanders.

Herbicide warfare grew steadily in rough proportion to the overall U.S. involvement in the Vietnam war between 1961 and 1967. However, by 1967, countervailing pressure had begun to constrain this growth. First, the military demand for herbicide threatened to outstrip domestic productive capacity. Second, pacification specialists within the United States Mission to Vietnam were alarmed by negative effects of the spray effort on their programs. Third, important segments of the U.S. scientific community expressed concern that massive herbicide use could lead to permanent distortion of Vietnamese ecosystems. Fourth, the idea that herbicide warfare was proscribed by the Geneva Protocol on Chemical and Biological Warfare (CBW) began to gain support in the international community. Later, scientists also were disturbed by evidence that certain herbicide agents might be deleterious to health.

The emergent criticism of herbicide warfare was coincident with the development of a strong and generalized protest movement against the war. Inevitably, the criticism of herbicide warfare on its own merits became to some extent intermingled and confused with its criticism as an element of "a dirty imperialistic war." Realistic analysis of the herbicide program within the government became difficult; open, productive dialogue between the government and outside groups became virtually impossible.

The Nixon Administration's decisions to de-escalate the Vietnam war and to review United States CBW policy have established a climate more conducive to an informed and rational examination of the American experience with herbicide warfare. Such examination must bring to bear not only the expertise of the soldier and the diplomat, but also the skills of the scientist, the economist, and the politician. This paper suggests relevant considerations for such a study.

It is not sufficient to define the issues. The pressure of events —in particular the impending resubmission of the Geneva

Protocol to the Senate—requires that the policy issue be reviewed carefully. Is the United States to retain or to relinquish its herbicide warfare capability? Much information relevant to the cost-effectiveness of the program is not presently available, although it might be developed. Hence the conclusions drawn in this paper are necessarily tentative. They are suggestive, not prescriptive, in intent.

Military Use of Herbicides

Level of Operations

The military potential of chemical herbicides has been recognized since they were first developed under United States Army contract during the Second World War. By 1960, a few chemical herbicides had been standardized and tested by the Army Chemical Corps. These were suggested as a possible means of denying the protection of jungle cover to the Viet Cong guerrillas. After considerable debate at high levels, President Kennedy authorized field testing, which began in 1961. The results of the field tests pleased the American command in South Vietnam, which had been searching for technological breakthroughs to assist in arresting the growing insurgency. In May 1963, an article in the semiofficial journal *Army* reported:

> Chemicals now in operational use in the Republic of Viet-Nam are effective against all types of vegetation of military interest. . . . A new weapon has been added to the fight against guerrillas. This weapon removes the leaves from the vegetation that the VC use to hide their presence. The resulting improvement in visibility should permit the more effective application of the superior combat power of the [Vietnamese Army].[3]

Until 1965, only modest, though steadily increasing, quantities of herbicides were employed, principally to reduce vegetation along lines of communication and in the vicinity of friendly camps. The Vietnamese Air Force may have also on occasion attacked crops in Viet Cong-dominated areas with herbicides; until mid-1964 such use was viewed dimly by top American officials. In 1965, coincident with the introduction of American ground forces, the United States greatly stepped up herbicide warfare. The mangrove swamp between Saigon and the sea was defoliated to hinder attacks on cargo vessels. This operation has often been cited as a very successful application of the weapon. Attacks on other large targets, especially the enemy strongholds to the north and east of Saigon, followed. By 1967-1969, the United States was using two dozen C-123s to spray about one-tenth of the total forested area of South Vietnam each year. However, since late 1969, "a lessening need for such missions due to improved pacification in the countryside" and budgetary constraints had led, by March 1970, to a 25 per cent cutback from 1969 levels.[4]

Table 1

Comparison of Chemical Defoliation and Anti-Crop
Operations in South Vietnam
1962 to July 1969

Year	Defoliation* (acres)	Crop (acres)	Per cent crop versus defoliation
1962	4,940	741	5
1963	24,700	247	1
1964	83,486	10,374	12
1965	155,610	65,949	42
1966	741,247	103,987	14
1967	1,486,446	221,312	15
1968	1,267,110	63,726	5
1969 (January-July)	797,180	38,819	5
TOTAL	4,560,719	505,155	

Source: U.S., Congress, House of Representatives, Committee on Foreign Affairs, Subcommittee on National Security Policy and Scientific Developments. *Chemical-Biological Warfare: U.S. Policies and International Effects* (Washington: U.S. Government Printing Office, 1970), p. 242.

* The total land area of South Vietnam is approximately 42 million acres. Of this, about 7.6 million acres is reported to be under intensive cultivation, and about 14 million acres is forested. About 25 per cent of the acreage sprayed in recent years is retreatment of previously sprayed areas.

A month later the Defense Department suspended use of Agent ORANGE pending the results of studies of its effect on animal life, thus reducing, at least temporarily, the spray program to 10–15 per cent of its 1969 level.[5]

Tactics

By the late 1960s, herbicide operations were an integral element of the U.S. effort in Vietnam. The herbicide program was sporadically chronicled in major American newspapers. While the Defense Department did not draw attention to the weapon, it readily provided factual information when questioned. Official spokesmen emphasized that the program was clearly beneficial to American objectives. For example, in August 1968, a statement by the United States Mission to Vietnam held that "the military benefits in terms of lives saved and other factors have far outweighed certain known adverse economic effects."[6] Similarly, the Defense Department wrote to Congressman Richard D. McCarthy in early 1969 that the "use of defoliants . . . to remove leaves from jungle foliage to reduce the threat of ambush and to increase visibility for U.S. forces . . . has saved many American and South Vietnamese lives."[7]

In December 1969, an extended rationale for the military use of herbicides was given in hearings before a subcommittee of the House Foreign Affairs Committee.[8] Rear Admiral William E. Lemos, the Defense Department spokesman, described five uses of chemical herbicides in Vietnam:

1. Defoliation of friendly base perimeters. Such clearance is generally performed by ground or helicopter spray. "This clearance opens fields of fire and affords observation for outposts to prevent surprise attack. . . . Without the use of herbicides around our fire bases, adequate defense is difficult and in many cases impossible."

2. Defoliation of lines of communication, especially "ambush sites" and "VC tax collection points." This tactic was "very effective in opening these areas so that they can be seen from observation aircraft, and with few ex-

ceptions, these roads were opened to free travel. . . .
[Herbicides are valuable] in preventing costly ambush of
army convoys." Similar defoliation is done along the
banks of navigable rivers and canals.

3. Defoliation of enemy infiltration routes to improve
aerial surveillance capability, "probably the most valuable use of herbicides for defoliation."

4. Defoliation of enemy base areas, "in order to make
him move in order to avoid exposing himself to aerial
observation."

5. Destruction of crops known to be grown by or for the
Viet Cong. This effort "in certain instances" has forced
the enemy "to divert tactical units from combat missions
to food procurement" and in areas of severe shortage has
stimulated defections.

In his testimony, Admiral Lemos quoted ranking American field commanders' comments on herbicide operations in
recent years. Defoliation was said to be "effective in enhanc-
ing" or to have "contributed significantly to" combat operations, especially by improving road security and by easing
reconnaissance.

A March 1970 newspaper article quotes "official sources"
in Saigon as saying that "future defoliation missions will con-
centrate less on cropland. The emphasis," it continued, "is
now on deep jungle infiltration routes and sanctuary areas
and on the jungle and brush surrounding American and South
Vietnamese fire bases and similar installations."[9] The newspaper story quoted "officers at U.S. headquarters" in Saigon
as considering "continued defoliation of infiltration routes . . .
vital." "This is particularly true," they said, "of the sometimes
triple-canopy jungle stretching north of Saigon into Cambodia
and in the north of the country around the A Shau Valley and
west of Hue and Da Nang." However, a field study by American scientists in August 1970 found that large-area spray
projects had virtually ceased after the use of Agent ORANGE
was suspended, so that while the overall program was mark-

edly reduced, anti-crop missions were a much higher percentage of the total.

Crop Destruction

The crop destruction effort, which in 1968-1969 accounted for about 5 per cent of the total spray delivered, is the most dubious aspect of the herbicide program. In the House Foreign Affairs Subcommittee hearings, Admiral Lemos was vigorously questioned on this tactic. He testified that targets were carefully selected by means of aerial photography and intelligence derived from Vietnamese in or near the target areas.

> Admiral Lemos: There has to be substantial evidence that crops are being grown specifically for the use of the Viet Cong troops and North Vietnamese troops.
>
> Mr. Fraser: And nobody else?
>
> Admiral Lemos: And nobody else.
>
> Mr. Fraser: Isn't that a very high standard to impose?
>
> Admiral Lemos: Yes, sir, and that is why the percentage of crop destruction is—a note just handed to me says: "Every year since we began the program, crop destruction has been less than 1 percent of the total South Vietnamese food production." It is not a large program.

The United States Army doctrine, based on international law, allows chemical destruction of crops "intended solely for consumption by the [enemy] Armed Forces (if that fact can be determined)."[10] Clearly this determination is difficult in the Vietnam war, and thus use of the tactic has been constrained, especially since 1967, when a review concluded that much chemical crop destruction caused civilian suffering without substantially hurting the Viet Cong. No matter how much care is taken, friendly intelligence is rarely sophisticated enough to make the fine discrimination between the "Viet Cong" and civilian crops, unless the United States and other allied forces in Vietnam tacitly accept the doctrine that civilians who willingly (or even grudgingly) support the enemy are "combatants."

Field commanders clearly consider herbicides of value in certain situations. "Target acquisition," or finding the enemy, has been a chronic problem in the Vietnam conflict. Reduction of foliage makes it more difficult for the enemy to avoid detection. Further, herbicides are relatively cheap. The current extensive use of herbicides in Vietnam is an understandable—perhaps even predictable—outcome of the problems facing the U.S. commanders, their perception of these problems, and the resources at their disposal.

Were target acquisition the only objective, 100 per cent defoliation would probably be desirable. No one advocates this, of course, since at some point the effect on popular loyalties, economic conditions, the ecological balance, and so forth will obviously outweigh any possible tactical gains. The objective is to find the optimum balance between military benefits and dysfunctional side effects. A rough balance is established by ensuring that all interested parties have appropriate control over the programming of spray missions. Such institutionalized checks, particularly the growing sensitivity of Vietnamese province chiefs to the possibility of inadvertent crop damage, are perhaps the best safeguard against the excesses that, a few years ago, stimulated much concern in Vietnam.

It is difficult to quantify the military gains derived from the spray program. It is possible to assemble precise information on the number and type of missions flown in an area and to chart trends in sightings of suspicious phenomena. It is also possible to count the number of engagements with enemy forces in an area, or the number of defectors, to screen prisoner interrogations for evidence, as well as to observe that vertical visibility improves in sprayed areas by 60 to 90 per cent and ground visibility by a lesser amount. But it is not easy to demonstrate a strong causal relationship among these phenomena. Quantification is hindered by the difficulty of holding constant over a period of time such factors as friendly and enemy strategies, troop deployments, or the influence of the weather. For example, a decrease in ambushes or apparent infiltration may result from a change in enemy objectives or an increase in sightings from more intensive reconnaissance; an increase in the defector rate could stem from a relaxation of enemy discipline or from heavy casualties, and so forth. Finally, it has to be remembered that distortions occur in even the most carefully crafted reporting systems.

The few statistics that have been reported to date are disappointing, and unlikely to convince a skeptical analyst.

a. During his appearance before the subcommittee of the House Foreign Affairs Committee in December 1969, Admiral Lemos testified that: "Major defoliation has been accomplished in War Zone C. Prior to defoliation, 7 brigades were necessary to maintain US/GVN [Government of Vietnam] presence. During 1967, after defoliation only 3 brigades were required."[11] Seven brigades were employed in Operation Junction City, a sweep of the enemy "war zone" in early 1967. Once the area was "neutralized," through destruction of enemy installations by ground troops and the construction of landing zones, fire bases, and roads for friendly use, it was possible to leave a smaller force in the area.[12] In other words, defoliation was but a part of the "treatment" intended to neutralize the area, not the cause of its neutralization.

b. Another House subcommittee was recently told that: "Complaints of inadvertent damage to the crops of friendly civilians, which earlier had numbered some 30 a month, had been reduced to 3 a month by early 1969." The first few months of the year are the middle of the dry season in southern Vietnam; few complaints should be expected.[13]

c. Two studies of enemy activity patterns in defoliation target areas before and after spraying were done some years ago. In one, a fourteen-kilometer stretch of highway, a 68 per cent decrease in enemy-initiated incidents was recorded. Additionally, "a definite shift in emphasis" away from hamlets and villages toward military installations occurred. The second case study, of two stretches of river, suggests that defoliation may have caused the enemy to shift from sustained attacks to harassing fire. Hence, although incidents were twice as numerous they were of reduced intensity.[14]

There is clearly a need for more extensive and careful

analysis. Sensitive analysts, using the sophisticated information collection and evaluation systems which have been developed by the U.S. military command in Vietnam in recent years, could probably assemble more persuasive data. In particular, analysts must ask what other phenomena can explain observed results. For example, in the highway study reported above, was a pacification campaign or some other development present that might have induced the enemy to shift mainforce units elsewhere? Or, in judging the effect of large-area defoliation, analysts might attempt to measure the degree to which spray operations, denuding about one-tenth of the forested area at any given time, have imposed logistical hardships on the enemy. It would be helpful to have more precise measures of the importance of defoliation to the overall reconnaissance effort. Intuitively, for example, the employment of both herbicides and electronic sensors is advantageous, but if it were necessary to rely on sensors alone, would surveillance capability be reduced on the order of 10 per cent or 90 per cent?[15] To what degree does defoliation force the enemy to relocate to less threatening positions rather than simply redirecting his effort against equally important friendly targets in unsprayed areas? Finally, careful analysis might seek to establish the level of spray operations that results in the maximum military advantage with the least expenditure of herbicide, or alternatively with the least dysfunctional side effects.

During the ten-year history of defoliation as a military tactic, the programming of operations has been governed more by the availability of agents and delivery systems, the influence of interested parties, and the political liabilities seen as associated with it than by careful study of its effect on the specific problems it is intended to overcome. Despite the inherent difficulty of developing meaningful quantitative data, it is to the advantage of all concerned that such an effort be made. Only with a more exact measure of the spray program's costs and benefits is it possible to assess properly the program in its broader policy context.

Side Effects

Examination of the herbicide program must consider the costs as well as gains to the war effort. First, there are direct costs: side effects that have a demonstrably negative impact on the military situation. Second, there are indirect costs: the less tangible linkage between U.S. herbicide warfare and American and foreign opinion with regard to the Vietnam war.

Even from a military point of view, defoliation has some drawbacks. It takes many days to act, and hence alerts the enemy to the possibility of impending operations. However popular herbicides are with the pilots of reconnaissance aircraft, some infantrymen regard the spray program as a mixed blessing. Defoliation of a double- or triple-canopy jungle increases the amount of sunlight reaching ground level; in time this greatly stimulates the growth of vines, bamboo, and other impediments to movement.

Defoliation and the Pacification Program

The principal argument against defoliation, from a tactical viewpoint, is its impact upon the pacification program. With varying degrees of emphasis, "political warfare" has been a key element of allied strategy in Vietnam. It is best described, perhaps, by the cliché, "winning hearts and minds," or, in any event, denying them to the enemy. Political warfare concepts undergird a broad spectrum of programs undertaken by the government of the Republic of Vietnam with U.S. advice and assistance, collectively known as "pacification."

Defoliation/crop destruction efforts have had a pronounced negative impact on the Vietnamese rural population. Vietnamese farmers have been alienated not only by actual accidental or deliberate damage to their crops but also by the threat of such damage. The failure, in most cases, of the indemnification mechanism has compounded the problem. This may be offset to some extent by appreciation of the increased security resulting from defoliation of roads and canals.

Precise estimates are not available, but it may be said that unintended agricultural damage has occurred on a large scale. Surveys in heavily populated provinces of the III Corps area (which received a disproportionately large proportion of spray missions) revealed that almost all farmers knew of damage to "friendly" crops and most believed that their own crops had been affected by herbicides. They often alleged, in addition, that the spray made children, chickens, and pigs ill and sometimes killed them. Such attitudes were said to be "common knowledge." The general population did not accept explanations that the program was designed to make the Viet Cong suffer; a frequent comment was to the effect that "we see no starving Viet Cong, but *our* life is terrible because of the defoliants." Payment of claims is not an adquate index of such damages, for the unwieldy claims system was swamped, at least since 1965-1968, with more or less verifiable reports of damages. There is evidence that the great majority of aggrieved farmers, believing—justifiably—that they had little chance of compensation, have not filed claims. Those charged with the administration of the indemnification program, on the other hand, have been exasperated by the high incidence of claims that seem to be false or grossly inflated.

A few years ago, pacification advisors were quite disturbed at the rising volume of complaints from farmers. Agricultural advisors and other specialists were able to cite example after example of inadvertent damage to civilian crops and wondered if the military benefits of the herbicide program could possibly outweigh the costs. Not until July 1967, when the U.S. civilian and military pacification programs were merged, was this criticism effective. The formation of CORDS (Civil Operations/Revolutionary Development Support, the central U.S. pacification agency, which is a branch of the military command) coincided with a program of large area defoliation north and east of Saigon. Complaints not only from farmers, but also the more articulate French rubber planters, led to a Mission-wide review of herbicide policy, conducted sporadically from November 1967 to August 1968. This review is important, for it seems to be the only broad analysis of the herbicide program undertaken within the United States government to date.

The U.S. Mission Committee on Herbicide Policy considered most of the significant problems: the military utility of herbicides, the spray program's effect on pacification and the Vietnamese economy, evidence of lasting ecological damage, the elaborate system for screening proposed missions, and the program's psychological warfare support—especially the indemnification mechanism. The central issue, however, was the controllability of herbicide delivery. Suggestions that herbicide vapor was drifting—or in some instances, being delivered —off-target had been a bone of contention for some time. Chemical Corps scientists held that the problem had been exaggerated. Pacification managers reported evidence of substantial damage to sensitive plants up to fifteen kilometers from where missions were said to have been flown. The review committee could not resolve the conflict and, in its report, straddled it. Its report noted the problem, incorporated the papers produced by the army scientists as appendices, and called on the military command to tighten up its operational controls and to engage a full-time plant pathologist. Wider buffer zones had earlier been drawn around the rubber plantations; after consideration, it was decided not to do the same with respect to other "friendly" crops. More significantly, since the committee was unable to resolve the scientific question (controllability), it had difficulty deciding the policy question: To what extent the conventional military gains from the herbicide program are vitiated by damage to the pacification program.

Post-review evidence indicates that inadvertent damage to friendly crops remains a problem despite stricter operating controls. For example, two scientists, G. H. Orians and E. W. Pfeiffer, reported that "every Vietnamese biologist we talked to [during a two-week stay in Vietnam] explained that herbicide damage has been frequent and regular over much of the delta region."[16] Similarly, an official United States investigating team has confirmed Cambodian charges of drift and/or overflight spray damage in broad areas well inside that country.[17]

Economic and Ecological Considerations

Analysis of the herbicide program should also consider

economic effects. Again, quantification is quite difficult. Some small fraction of the inflation of food prices and the localized shortages may be attributable to the spray program. In addition to actual herbicide damage to fruit and vegetable crops, attitude surveys suggest that some farmers have refrained from raising certain crops from fear of such damage. It would be easier to estimate the effect of herbicide programs on rubber production, as both the plantations and Vietnamese government offices maintain careful records. Rubber provided about 40 per cent of the nation's prewar export earnings. According to Orians and Pfeiffer, the Vietnamese Rubber Research Institute believed in 1969 that "repeated defoliations [were] creating a threat to the very existence of rubber culture in Viet-Nam."[18] Fairly accurate estimates of losses in timber should also be feasible. Against this should be balanced economic gains realized from increased security of roads and waterways due to defoliation.

Long-term ecological and health costs are much more difficult to calculate but could be of great importance. The question of ecological damage has been raised by a number of American scientists and by the American Association for the Advancement of Science (AAAS). Among the specific ecological dangers that have been cited are laterization (irreversible hardening) of the soil, permanent destruction of mangrove associations and attendant loss of aquatic protein resources, destruction of timber resources, depletion of soil nutrients by leaching of deforested areas, and invasion of herbicide-treated regions by bamboo and grasses. The very few direct observations made to date suggest that laterization is not a substantial problem but that destruction of mangrove associations and overgrowth by bamboo and grasses has been extensive. Whether or not major soil depletion has occurred is not presently known. In order to define and quantify these and other possible ecological consequences, the AAAS in January 1970 created an "herbicide assessment commission" with the intention of conducting a broad study of the effects of herbicides on the ecology of Vietnam and on public health.

Concern that the herbicides used in Vietnam may be hazardous to health has come to the fore only recently, following the appearance of laboratory studies suggesting that 2,4-D and 2,4,5-T (ingredients of the herbicides most commonly used in Vietnam), may be teratogenic (fetus-damaging) to man. These findings led the U.S. Office of Science and Technology to announce late in 1969 a series of restrictions on the use of 2,4,5-T within the United States. At the same time it was announced that the Department of Defense would restrict the use of 2,4,5-T to areas remote from the population. However, doubts about the initial laboratory studies delayed the implementation of domestic restriction. No epidemiological study of the matter has been reported; accordingly, it is not known whether or not 2,4,5-T has caused birth defects in Vietnam. Finally, in April 1970 following further laboratory evidence that 2,4,5-T is teratogenic, the domestic use of the herbicide in the United States was severely restricted and the Office of the Deputy Secretary of Defense announced that the use of Agent ORANGE, which contains 2,4,5-T, had been suspended pending an evaluation. Other herbicides were said to be available as substitutes.[19]

On the one hand, government spokesmen have generally minimized the possibility of health hazards and ecological damage in Vietnam by pointing out that the same chemicals are commonly used for domestic purposes in the United States. On the other hand, statements emanating from Hanoi and from the National Liberation Front have alleged large-scale herbicide poisoning of humans, farm animals, and fish. Although Vietnamese Communist claims are certainly issued with propaganda effects in mind they should not be dismissed out of hand. There have also been occasional claims of toxic effects in the South Vietnamese press and legislature and, as noted above, such beliefs seem to be widely held among the rural population. The fact that herbicides are used domestically in the United States is not necessarily relevant to the Vietnamese situation. In the United States, cacodylic acid, picloram, and 2,4,5-T are not licensed for general use on food crops. Residues of 2,4-D in the American diet are systematically monitored and occur rarely and then only at an extremely low level. The amount of herbicides used per acre in Vietnam is generally far higher than that used for domestic purposes. It is not known what concentrations of herbicide chemicals enter the diet of the Vietnamese population as a result of direct consumption of exposed vegetation or as a result of drinking contaminated water. Whether or not the ingestion of moderate quantities of any of these chemicals is harmful to human health is not known at present. The area is one of increasingly active experimentation and investigation in the United States. Thus, while there is no definite evidence of major ecological or health damage caused by herbicides in Vietnam, aside from the destruction of mangrove associations and invasion of hardwood forests by grasses, further study is clearly warranted.

Psychological Considerations

Finally, there is the emotional impact of the herbicide program on the Vietnamese population. This, too, is relevant to the war effort. Defoliation is viewed by Vietnamese as an American program, official fictions notwithstanding. The rural population does not readily accept explanations that the program is designed to hurt the Viet Cong; it does see that it makes life more difficult for the farmer. Nor are adverse psychological effects confined to the farming population, as an excerpt from a very popular contemporary memoir, *Requiem for Hue (Tinh Ca cho Hue Do Nat)* illustrates:

> I entered the gate, and looked about the orchard. . . . The trees were nearly all dry and dead. The big front yard, which in former years had been filled with heavy-laden orange and guava trees, now was overgrown with grass of a sickly yellow color. My younger sister explained sadly, "The herbicide killed all the trees."
>
> She pointed at the tips of the coconut palms. "You can see. A year ago when we came back after the fighting stopped, I was able to pick a few nuts to drink the milk. This year there were no nuts."
>
> The palms had not been strong enough to put out new leaves; the young nuts were dried and shriveled just like betel nuts. I looked across the pond, now dry, at the yellow plum tree. At Tet a year ago, even though the air had been heavy with the smoke of guns and the stench of blood, still it had bloomed profusely, gilding the entire pond. This Spring it bore but a few dried leaves and a rare green one, not a single blossom.

Domestic Political Costs

In the United States, criticism of the use of herbicides in the Vietnam war has come from diverse sources. At one extreme, "doves" have emphasized the moral issue; they hold in particular that a strategy of food denial is repugnant and criminal, arguing that it affects the civilian population long before soldiers go on short rations. Arms control advocates have emphasized the challenge to international bans and inhibitions against chemical and biological weapons inherent in the employment of herbicides. Finally, natural scientists have evidenced a deeply felt concern over the use of herbicide weapons on a massive scale while the potential effects of such use on the environment and on human life remain inadequately understood. Late in the 1960s, the scientists became the most effective and persistent antagonists of herbicide warfare, and their dominant concerns have been the focal points of the domestic debate. Thus, for a time the controversy, as relayed to the general public, seemed to turn exclusively on the possibility of long-term ecological damage to Vietnam. Subsequently, the possibility of teratogenic (fetus-damaging) and other directly detrimental effects on human beings has been raised.

The military herbicide program's cost in terms of weakened domestic support for the war has to date been limited to its effect on a few key groups—especially scientists and conservationists. President Richard Nixon's non-inclusion of herbicides (and tear gases) on the proscribed list in his statement on chemical and biological warfare of 25 November 1969 has focused additional attention on these chemical agents.

As the Senate moves to consider ratification of the Geneva Protocol, which President Nixon requested on 19 August 1970, it seems likely that the American herbicide warfare program, even in its present curtailed form, will be subject to considerable additional criticism. The Administration's position is that the Protocol "does not ban the use of . . . defoliating herbicides . . . as now employed in the Indochina war."[20] In what may be a litmus test of Senate sentiment, the upper house in late August rejected an amendment to the FY 1971 military procurement bill which would have barred U.S. military use of herbicides (by 22 votes in favor, 62 against), and also a narrower proposal, which sought only to ban military use of herbicides on food crops in Vietnam (by 33 votes in favor, 48 against).

Diplomatic Costs

The diplomatic costs of herbicide warfare are also significant. The United Nations and the Eighteen Nation Committee on Disarmament (ENDC)—now the Conference of the Committee on Disarmament—have paid increased attention to CBW in recent years. This interest has been stimulated by the tendency of the "nuclear club" to handle nuclear problems among themselves, by the rapid progress of the natural sciences, by reports of poison gas warfare in Yemen, and finally, by the employment of tear gas and herbicides in Vietnam. The Geneva Protocol of 1925, which alone among the interwar disarmament agreements survived the Second World War, has—rationally or not —acquired a powerful mystique and, in the eyes of some, the force of customary international law. The diplomatic/legal trend in recent years, drawing on escalation theory, has been toward advocacy of an absolute ban on the use of chemical and biological weapons. U.S. arguments that proscription of herbicides does not fall within the language of the Protocol have become increasingly unpopular.

Not until late 1966, some four and one-half years after the first reports of herbicide testing in Vietnam, did North Vietnam's allies confirm State Department predictions by raising the issue in the United Nations General Assembly. At that time a rather propagandistic Hungarian resolution was successfully watered down by the United States and its allies to an expression of support for "the principles and objectives" of the Protocol and a call for adherence to it. Although it was evident from the United Nations General Assembly debate that there was significant concern over U.S. use of tear gas and herbicides in Vietnam, less than one-fifth of the United Nations non-Communist membership was sufficiently aroused to support an oblique condemnation of the United States.

In 1968 the General Assembly commissioned an "experts'

report" on CBW. This mater-of-fact discussion of the likely present and future characteristics of CBW was transmitted to the membership in July 1969. A foreword by Secretary-General Thant urged:

> A clear affirmation that the prohibition contained in the Geneva Protocol applies to the use in war of all chemical, bacteriological and biological agents (including tear gas and other harassing agents) which now exist or may be developed in the future.[21]

There can be little doubt that the experts' report played a key role in crystallizing opinion in the General Assembly. Evidently, much of this information, although available in the United States, was a revelation to many of the delegations. It was characteristically termed "an eye-opener," "remarkable," and "thought-provoking" in subsequent debate. The report solidified a vague uneasiness about CBW; U Thant's recommendation became a focal point for the expression of that uneasiness.

As a result, despite U.S. protests that the experts had no legal or diplomatic competence to interpret the Protocol, and that "it would be a grave error for the General Assembly to adopt a new practice now of interpreting treaties by majority vote,"[22] and despite President Nixon's restatement of U.S. policy on CBW on 25 November 1969, the United States found itself isolated at the twenty-fourth United Nations General Assembly. By a vote of 58 to 3[23] in the First (political and security) Committee, and 80 to 3 in the General Assembly, it was held that the use of all chemical and biological weapons "which might be employed because of their direct toxic effect on man, animals and plants" was contrary to international law. There were, to be sure, thirty-five abstentions, including thirteen NATO members and most of the Asian allies of the United States. However, it is difficult to escape the conclusion that this vote was a rather sharp rebuff to the U.S. interpretation of the Geneva Protocol. Examination of the statements of the abstaining states suggests that if the competence of the United Nations to interpet the Protocol had not been an issue and/or if a positive vote on the resolution would not have implied desertion of a major ally, support for the broader interpretation would have been nearly universal. Delegates who have defended the U.S. position at international arms control discussions have reported strong private criticism of the American stand by the representatives of NATO allies and other friendly states.[24]

Arms Control Costs

Use of chemical weapons by the United States in Vietnam was instrumental in sensitizing the United Nations to the problem of CBW. It does not necessarily follow, however, that this concern will dissipate when the Vietnam war ends. The U.S. position with respect to tear gases and herbicides conflicts with generally accepted concepts of arms control, that is, the problems of escalation and proliferation. Thus these agents, although not terribly dangerous *per se,* are of relevance to the larger issue of chemical and biological arms control. The "firebreak" concept, which has been developed in nuclear warfare studies, is also relevant to chemical weapons.

Experts may distinguish confidently between herbicides and "all other chemical weapons." It is not certain that such a distinction can be maintained by political or military leaders required to make rapid decisions in a fluid wartime environment, possibly with incomplete information. The rapid progress of the natural sciences threatens to further blur the distinctions between herbicides and other agents. Especially when there is no general agreement as to the legitimacy of herbicides as an instrument of warfare, their use entails a risk of unintended escalation to general CBW.

An herbicide warfare capability is within the reach of most nations. In the absence of general agreement to their proscription, other powers may also be tempted to employ them. One might wonder, in the light of the preceding discussion of the weapon's tactical utility in Vietnam, why herbicides would be so attractive. The temptation lies not in the relatively expensive tactic of defoliation—the reduction of vegetation to hinder movement of guerrilla-type forces — but in the still unplumbed possibilities of crop destruction. If the constraints that the United States has imposed on itself in its herbicide operations in Vietnam are not operative, ruinous assaults on crops such as rubber, cotton, or bananas become a real possibility. The developing nations, typically dependent on one or two cash crops, are disproportionately vulnerable to herbicide attack.[25] Should some states choose to develop an herbicide warfare capability, their neighbors may feel compelled to acquire their own system as a deterrent. Finally, it should be noted that once a military herbicide delivery system is acquired, it may stimulate and facilitate the acquisition of delivery systems for other chemical warfare agents.

It would seem, therefore, that U.S. employment of herbicide weapons in Vietnam has imposed significant diplomatic costs. Although foreign newspapers have not stressed "American chemical warfare," the United States has suffered some propaganda costs. American credibility with regard to general CBW arms control has been eroded. From a theoretical standpoint, United States efforts to distinguish herbicides from other chemical weapons are built on shaky premises, whatever the technical legality of the American interpretation of the Geneva Protocol. There is reason to believe that the United States position could lead to a proliferation of herbicide weapons and that this would be destabilizing in effect. Hence herbicide warfare appears to be to some extent prejudicial to larger American foreign policy interests.

Conclusions

The value of herbicides as military agents and that of defoliation and crop destruction as tactics depends largely on the military objectives sought. Review of the U.S. experience in Vietnam suggests that herbicide operations have been at cross-purposes with the political/psychological aims of "unconventional warfare." Herbicide operations seem to be of greater utility as an element of a "conventional" defensive strategy than as an element of an offensive strategy. The greatest benefits are probably obtained once populated areas are cleared of large enemy units and defoliants are employed only to create a broad "no-man's-land" in the unpopulated hinterlands. Under the self-imposed constraints on American crop destruction operations in the

Vietnam war, this tactic seems to have been counter-productive. The recent trend, ironically, has been to curb the use of defoliants (as a threat to health) while continuing crop destruction.

Examination of the public record does not reveal a conclusive case that United States "forces have been better able to accomplish their mission with significantly reduced U.S. and Vietnamese casualties." Besides, military gains have been vitiated to an uncertain extent by the evident economic and psychological costs in Vietnam. Beyond such general conclusions, the analyst is on highly conjectural ground, for a reliable data base does not exist at this point. The inherent problems of gathering meaningful statistics in Vietnam make quantitative analysis difficult. However, it is probably possible to provide a more objective foundation for policy choices than is now available.

Possible long-lasting damage to ecosystems and public health raise troubling questions of a moral nature and have imposed significant domestic political costs. Consideration of these and of evident diplomatic costs raises doubts as to the wisdom of retaining herbicides in the U.S. arsenal. Short-run American interests excepted, there is a demonstrable international interest in bringing these agents within the scope of the Geneva Protocol ban and reason to fear proliferation if this is not done. Herbicides thus present a significant policy dilemma. A substantial group of Senators will oppose any move to retain herbicides in the arsenal, or to keep them at least until the termination of hostilities in Vietnam. Should the Geneva Protocol be ratified with a reservation (or interpretation) excepting herbicides, some of the other parties may balk at accepting treaty relations with the United States, as a matter of either politics or principle. In any event, such a qualification would be a diplomatic liability. Finally, as U.S. forces are withdrawn from Vietnam, should the South Vietnamese be endowed with a spray capability?

The consequences of renouncing herbicides, at this juncture, are also troublesome. It may weaken the United States military posture in Southeast Asia. Certainly many believe this would be the case. Giving up the herbicide capability might also seem to some to be an implicit admission by the United States that the use of these agents in Vietnam had been an infraction of international morality.

Nonetheless, policy develops in a dynamic context, and may gracefully be modified to accord with changing circumstances. As noted above, use of the most common agent has recently been suspended in the United States in light of laboratory tests indicating that such use may pose a public health hazard. Another agent is, for similar reasons, suspect. Electronic surveillance devices promise to accomplish in the foreseeable future some of the tasks which now require herbicides. Finally, renunciation of military herbicides is worth considering in the interest of securing greater uniformity of interpretation of the Geneva Protocol.

REFERENCES

1. U.S. Department of the Army, Training Circular TC 3-16, Apr. 1969, para. 51.

2. Three such agents have been in general use in the Vietnam conflict. "ORANGE," a mixture of 2, 4-D and 2, 4, 5-T, is most common. "WHITE," a mixture of 2, 4-D and picloram in a water base, is less volatile than ORANGE, and hence is used where drift damage to friendly crops is feared. These two agents are technically classed as "growth-regulating compounds." "BLUE," an aqueous solution of cacodylic acid, is classed as a dessicant. It is mainly used to destroy rice crops. For the sake of brevity, these agents will be referred to collectively in this paper as "herbicides."

3. LTC Stanley D. Fair, "No Place to Hide," *Army*, Sept. 1963.

4. *Los Angeles Times,* 11 Mar. 1970.

5. *Washington Post,* 23 June 1970.

6. Statement of the United States Mission, September 1968, reprinted in Richard D. McCarthy, *The Ultimate Folly* (New York: Vintage, 1969), pp. 92–93.

7. Ibid.

8. U.S. Congress, House of Representatives, Committee on Foreign Affairs, Subcommittee on National Security Policy and Scientific Developments. *Chemical-Biological Warfare: U.S. Policies and International Effects* (Washington: U.S. Government Printing Office, 1970), pp. 223–254 (hereafter cited as Zablocki Subcommittee Hearings).

9. Ibid., footnote 3.

10. United States Department of the Army, *The Law of Land Warfare,* Field Manual FM 27-10, para. 38, pp. 18–19.

11. Zablocki Subcommittee Hearings, op. cit., p. 231.

12. LTG Richard G. Stilwell, "Evolution in Tactics—The Vietnam Experience," *Army,* Feb. 1970, p. 18.

13. U.S., Congress, House, Committee on Science and Astronautics, Subcommittee on Science, Research and Development. *A Technology Assessment of the Vietnam Defoliant Matter* (Washington, D.C.: U.S. Gov't. Printing Office, 1969), p. 20.

14. Data supplied to the author by Office of the Secretary of Defense.

15. Electronic sensors have been highly touted as "surveillance devices that can continually track the enemy," which "should revolutionize the battlefield of the future." *New York Times,* 15 Oct. 1969, and 13 Feb. 1970. Sensors have been in operational use in Vietnam for several years; few, however, believe that they are an adequate substitute for aerial defoliation in their present state of development.

16. G. H. Orians and E. W. Pfeiffer, "Mission to Vietnam, Part 1," *Scientific Research,* 9 June 1969, p. 30.

·62

17. Minarik, et al., "A Report on Herbicide Damage to Rubber and Fruit Trees in Cambodia," Saigon, 12 July 1969.
18. Orians and Pfeiffer, "Mission to Vietnam," op. cit.
19. *Washington Post,* 16 Apr. 1970.
20. *Washington Post,* 20 Aug. 1970.
21. *Chemical and Bacteriological (Biological) Weapons and Effects of their Possible Use,* United Nations Pub. Sales No. E.69.I.24, p. xii.
22. UN Doc. A/C.1/PV. 1717, 10 Dec. 1969, p. 17.
23. The United States, Australia, and Portugal voted against this resolution, both in the Committee and the Assembly.
24. See Zablocki Subcommittee Hearings, op. cit., pp. 56, 58, 71, 126.
25. The relative sensitivity of a variety of tropical crops to herbicides is discussed in Minarik, et al., op. cit.

THE MILITARY VALUE AND POLITICAL IMPLICATIONS OF THE USE OF RIOT CONTROL AGENTS IN WARFARE

by Stewart Blumenfeld and Matthew Meselson

In November 1969, President Richard Nixon enunciated United States chemical warfare policies that made it clear that a basic United States objective was the elimination of biological and chemical weapons from the arsenals of the world. He announced a unilateral halt in all U.S. activities in the field of offensive biological warfare, reaffirmed that the United States would not use lethal chemicals except in retaliation, and proposed to seek Senate approval for ratification of the Geneva Protocol. While the President made no official pronouncement on the use of riot control or harassing chemical agents, it was indicated afterward that the United States government did not include such agents in the category of proscribed chemicals. Similarly, the President made no references to such chemicals when he submitted the Protocol to the Senate on 19 August 1970, but Secretary of State William P. Rogers' report accompanying this submission stated that "it is the United States understanding of the Protocol that it does not prohibit the use in war of riot control agents."

Over the past five years, U.S. military forces in Vietnam have been making increasing use of the riot control agent CS. Initially the only munition available was the standard hand grenade designed for use in crowd control. It was supplied with the announced expectation that its use would be confined to defensive and rescue operations and to situations where enemy soldiers were intermingled with noncombatants. However, once CS was used in Vietnam, chemical staffs as well as regular soldiers and field commanders found a widening variety of roles for it. Under pressure from the battlefield, new types of CS munitions were developed and came to be applied over a wide range of combat operations.

In parallel with the increased combat use of CS in Vietnam, there has been increasing concern over the possible long-term arms control and political costs to the United States of maintaining its option to use harassing agents in war. Thus, on the one hand, CS is militarily useful against the enemy in Vietnam, but, on the other hand, any use of gas in war, even riot control agents, is a departure from the long-standing policy of the major powers to avoid the initiation of gas warfare of any kind. Furthermore, a large number of parties to the Geneva Protocol of 1925, which prohibits the use of gas warfare, have asserted that in their opinion, it does apply to riot control agents.[1] The arms control risks of using riot control agents arise from the resultant stimulation of worldwide military interest in the potential of chemical warfare and from the possibility of battlefield escalation from these agents to more toxic chemicals.

Thus, although there is no great difficulty in identifying qualitatively the opposing gains and costs of using riot control agents in war, there is a very difficult problem in attempting to quantify the various considerations and then to place values on them in order to reach conclusions. This paper attempts to bring additional perspective to the various considerations described above.

Background on the Military Use of Harassing Chemicals

Chemical warfare in the modern sense was initiated at the very beginning of World War I. The chemicals first employed in World War I were tear gases and respiratory irritants which, in today's terminology, would be designated nonlethal.[2] This was not by intent, however, and more toxic chemicals soon issued from the laboratories of the warring powers and then were employed on the battlefields on a massive scale. Nevertheless, lachrymatory and irritant agents remained in use, since they could effectively harass unmasked personnel and force the wearing of gas masks at much lower concentrations than could the lethal agents. In all, 6,000 tons of lachrymators and 7,000 tons of respiratory irritant gases were expended by both sides during the First World War. Amos A. Fries (the then Chief of the U.S. Army Chemical Warfare Service) and Clarence J. West predicted that "so great is the harassing value of tear and irritant gases that the next war will see them used in quantities approximating that of the more poisonous gases."[3] They were mistaken; chemicals—both lethal and nonlethal—sat out the next two major wars.

Chloroacetophenone (CN) was developed in the United States near the end of World War I. The war ended before it could be used, but CN was thereafter adopted by many civilian police agencies as their standard tear gas. During World War II, CN grenades and other munitions were stockpiled by the United States, Germany, and Japan. A vomiting agent, diphenylchloroarsine (called Adamsite and designated DM), was also stockpiled by both sides. However, despite their availability, neither gas was used in the Second World War. In large measure, the reason for this avoidance of even nonlethal gases seems to have been that neither side could see a clear advantage in their introduction into the war; there was also a genuine repugnance to gas warfare on the part of many civilian and military leaders. According to Albert Speer, both of these reasons were instrumental in forestalling Germany's use of chemical weapons against the Allies late in 1944, even though the idea was proffered by Hitler himself.[4] No gas of any kind was used in combat in Korea. Although authorization for tear gas was occasionally requested, it was never granted.

Both CN and DM were used in the early days in Vietnam. Among the munitions supplied to the South Vietnamese army (ARVN) early in the course of U.S. involvement was a quantity of standard hand grenades containing CN and a CN-DM mixture. While these probably were intended for riot control, the ARVN made occasional military use of them, notably in flushing enemy personnel from caves and bunkers. However, employment of gas grenades was relatively infrequent and *ad hoc,* rather than integral to a tactical plan. CN and DM have now been almost completely superseded by CS.

CS munitions made a somewhat inauspicious debut in Vietnam in December 1964. On two occasions CS grenades were airdropped as part of an attempt to rescue U.S. prisoners of war. The results were inconclusive in that in neither case was contact actually made with the enemy. Early in 1965, the Commander of the U.S. Military Advisory Command in Vietnam directed American advisory teams to draw masks and CS grenades for their own defense. It was thought that in certain cases in which advisory teams had been overrun by the Viet Cong the last-ditch use of CS might have caused the Viet Cong to avoid an area large enough for the organization of effective counter-action.

In March 1965, *The New York Times* reported on the operational employment of nonlethal chemicals by the ARVN. The story quoted a U.S. spokesman as saying: "Even if it (the use of nonlethal chemicals) does work, there is a real problem in getting it accepted . . . the idea of it all brings back memories of World War I and mustard gas." The report provoked considerable controversy in the American and foreign press. The official attitude of the U.S. government, as conveyed by the statements of the then Secretary of State Dean Rusk and the then Secretary of Defense Robert McNamara, held that the United States and its allies were not in contravention of the principles of the Geneva Protocol, arguing that the chemical agents used were not war gases but riot control types of weapons. Moreover, Rusk stated that "we do not expect that gas will be used in ordinary military operations . . . the anticipation is, of course, that these weapons will be used only in those situations involving riot control or situations analogous to riot control."[5] For five months following this statement, U.S. forces in Vietnam did not employ riot control agents and a quiet effort was made to discourage South Vietnamese use of them. Simultaneously, an assessment of the pros and cons of employing riot control agents was conducted within U.S. military and political circles.

While this was going on, an event occurred that was probably more important in formulating subsequent policy than any government study. On 5 September 1965, the Commander of the 2nd Battalion, 7th Marine Regiment, faced with the problem of flushing a Viet Cong force out of a tunnel (in which he had reason to believe there were also women and children) elected to employ CS to help clear it. As a result, some 400 persons, including 17 armed Viet Cong, were removed without injury to the noncombatants. Since the use of CS was then contrary to Command policy, a Board of Inquiry was convened, but it eventually determined that the action taken had been in the best interest of all concerned.

Shortly thereafter, without any public announcement, a new policy sanctioning the expanded use of CS was settled upon, and CS in its various forms came to be regarded as a normal military weapon to be exploited operationally as deemed useful by field commanders, subject, of course, to the same constraints that pertain to other weapons and munitions.

Initially, it was expected that CS would be used primarily to reduce civilian casualties and the destruction of civilian property. Subsequently, however, the use of CS expanded rapidly to encompass a wide range of battlefield operations. The procurement for Southeast Asia of CS and its later forms, CS1 and CS2, rose very rapidly in fiscal year 1966, although it was significant even in fiscal year (FY) 1964 (Table 1). The differences between CS, CS1, and CS2 are discussed in the next section.

Table 1

Procurement of CS, CS1, and CS2 for Southeast Asia
(thousands of pounds)

	FY1964	FY1965	FY1966	FY1967	FY1968	FY1969
CS	225	93	378	437	714	2018
CS1	142	160	1217	770	3249	160
CS2	0	0	0	0	228	3885
Total	367	253	1595	1207	4191	6063

Source: *Congressional Record* H4775, 12 June 1969.

Agent CS and CS Munitions

The initial development of CS as a riot control agent was carried out in the United Kingdom in the early 1950s. The compound was named after B. B. Corson and R. W. Staughton, the American chemists who first reported its synthesis in 1928.

The technology was soon transmitted to the U.S. Army Chemical Corps and most research on the agent since then has been done under U.S. auspices.

CS, orthochlorobenzylidene malononitrile, is a whitish solid of low volatility. It is only slightly soluble in water. Exposure to CS results in severe irritation of the eyes, nose, and respiratory tract, with copious tearing and blepharospasm (involuntary closure of the eyes), racking cough, and a feeling of difficulty in breathing. High doses may result in nausea and vomiting. CS can also produce a somewhat painful stinging on damp skin, which is harassing but not by itself incapacitating. Intense exposure to CS under humid conditions can cause severe blistering that takes several days to heal. Individuals may become sensitized to the agent after an initial exposure.

One reason CS is useful as a military agent is that it produces incapacitation rapidly—in five to thirty seconds, depending upon the dose received. Incapacitation extends throughout the period of exposure, and for an additional one to ten minutes. The eye effects occur first, followed by the respiratory signs. Evidence from animal experimentation extrapolated to humans indicates that for CS the difference between an incapacitating exposure and one that might produce serious lasting effects is quite large, a factor of many thousands. Nevertheless, exposures in some cases in Vietnam may have exceeded the human lethal dosage estimated from laboratory experiments with animals, although no deaths resulting from the use of CS have been confirmed. It is not yet clear whether there have indeed been none, or if there have been some that have not been verified.

Depending upon a number of individual human variables, chiefly sensitivity and motivation, the combined effects of CS result in varying degrees of incapacitation. Unmasked troops who are exposed to CS for the first time or who are deficient in training and/or discipline may react by abandoning their positions, attempting to flee from the cloud. Experienced troops are less likely to leave their positions; nevertheless, under the influence of CS, their fighting proficiency will be considerably impaired. Unprotected troops forced to assault through a cloud of CS are likely to falter.

The original form of the agent is designated simply CS. It is mixed with a pyrotechnic material which, upon ignition, vaporizes the CS and ejects it through ports in the munition. In contact with the air, the vapor resolidifies into an aerosol cloud whose travel is entirely a function of air movement. This material has a low volatility and is inactivated by water and thus usually presents a negligible residual hazard. When it is used in an attack on an enemy position, it may be followed closely with an advance of unmasked troops, although a certain amount of caution is prudent because of the danger of lingering pockets of contaminated air. CS has been manufactured in two other forms—CS1 and CS2, both formulated specifically to produce an agent with high persistency. CS1, however, is considerably less persistent than CS2 and was really an interim development. While a great deal of CS1 was used in Vietnam from about 1966 to 1969, CS2, now that it is available in quantity, is considered the agent of choice. CS2 does not react readily with water, and effective concentrations will persist in caves, bunkers, and tunnels for several weeks. CS2, in fact, is so resistant to wetting that it can be placed on the surface of a small body of water, and any agitation of the surface (as by the wind or by wading) may generate an effective aerosol of CS.

The variety of CS munitions has increased substantially from the two ground and two aerial weapons available in 1966. Hand grenades, which are similar to those used domestically for riot control, are the basic infantry CS weapon. Also in widespread use is a 40-millimeter CS round for the M-79 grenade launcher. Other infantry weapons are the 4.2 inch chemical mortar, firing a shell that ejects four pyrotechnic submunitions, which burn on the ground to form a dense cloud of CS, the 105 millimeter CS howitzer projectile and the man-portable E8 rocket launcher, which fires a large number of skittering submunitions and is useful for submerging small structures in a cloud of CS to facilitate their assault by troops. High-capacity blowers are sometimes used to flush cave and tunnel complexes with CS2. Aerial disseminators and canister dispensers have been developed to enhance close air support of ground troops. Several bulk systems, such as 80-

pound drums with a burster charge, have been developed for terrain interdiction and area denial.

Only the U.S. forces in Vietnam have this variety of CS munitions at their disposal. The ARVN has a much more restricted capability, and the forces of other allied powers are limited in the main to hand grenades.

Defense Against CS

An effective gas mask, such as the U.S. standard M-17 or the newer, lightweight XM-28E4, provides adequate protection of the face and respiratory tract against CS. The Soviet Shlem mask is equally effective. The two-piece Communist Chinese mask affords a lower degree of protection but may suffice to mitigate the effects of light concentrations of CS. The Viet Cong field-expedient masks, which consist solely of a filter comprising several layers of gauze and cotton (sometimes with a small amount of charcoal), provide only minimal protection.

There is also a problem of protection against the skin-irritating effects of CS. Normal clothing, fairly tight-fitting around the neck, wrist, and ankles is adequate against light to moderate concentrations. Personnel with less protection (that is, wearing short pants and short sleeves) attempting to move through heavy concentrations of the agent will be considerably harassed, though in the case of well-motivated troops, probably not to the point of incapacitation.

Operational Employment of CS Munitions in Vietnam[6]

Area Denial

The largest part of the CS used in Vietnam has been dispensed as bulk CS1 or CS2 with the intention of denying the use of terrain or field fortifications to the enemy. Contamination of large parcels of terrain or of terrain not accessible to friendly ground troops is effected by means of air-delivered fifty-five gallon drums fitted with an explosive charge. Each of these releases eighty pounds of agent. The drums are dropped by helicopter, up to thirty per sortie, and are exploded just above the ground. The result is a roughly circular pattern of visible contamination, high enough in concentration to preclude habitation in the near vicinity. The targets, usually base camps, rest areas, or infiltration routes, are requested by divisional sub-elements, evaluated by the intelligence branch, and passed along for action to the division chemical staff. A survey in 1968 of division activity reports indicated that these missions constituted a major part of the effort of the chemical staffs.

Bulk CS1 or CS2 is also used to contaminate field fortifications such as bunkers, caves, and tunnels. This is sometimes more effective than the usual destructive methods for denying use of the facility to the enemy for several weeks or more. In these cases, the agent is either hand-sown or scattered by detonating a grenade inside a container of agent—often one of the small eight-pound polyethylene bags in which the chemical is shipped—or, if the space is fairly small, exploding a CS2 grenade in it. Sometimes CS will be combined with explosive destruction—on a bunker, for example—to retard renovation for reuse.

Offensive Combat Operations

CS munitions are also used in Vietnam in direct engagement of the enemy during offensive combat operations. These operations fall into several roughly distinct categories: assault against point targets; assault against area targets; flushing of bunkers, caves, and other structures; use in conjunction with antipersonnel artillery and air strikes; suppression of small arms fire around helicopter landing zones; and reduction of enemy resistance to facilitate taking prisoners or to minimize the danger to noncombatants in close proximity to resisting troops.

Typical point targets include single bunkers, automatic weapon emplacements, and small buildings. The preferred munition in these cases is often the 40-millimeter CS round for the M-79 grenade launcher. In the hands of a skilled grenadier, it can be fired through a window or port from a distance of 200 or 300 meters. Within a few seconds, any occupants lacking protection will be incapacitated.

CS munitions are also used to reduce friendly casualties when artillery support is either not available or impractical due to other considerations. U.S. Marines found the extensive employment of CS to be particularly desirable during the Battle of Hue in February 1968 while fighting in congested areas and assaulting fortified positions. In that battle, close contact between enemy and friendly troops (usually 20 to 150 meters), coupled with poor weather conditions, limited the use of artillery and air support, and forced the troops to depend largely on the organic weapons they had at hand. CS launchers and hand grenades were used as an effective alternate means of supporting the almost continual assaults on fortified positions and of routing the enemy from hallways and rooms in the many buildings.

As described in Army training manuals,[7] CS is also used in conjunction with artillery and air strikes. If the chemical agent is placed on the target immediately prior to bombardment with antipersonnel munitions, the enemy may be panicked into leaving his cover to escape the CS and thereby be rendered more vulnerable to conventional arms. There is good evidence that this tactic works against poorly disciplined troops. In an action against a well-entrenched enemy force on the Bon Son Plain in May 1967, the 1st Air Cavalry Division combined CS attacks with air strikes on the enemy position, followed closely by an infantry/tank assault. The action resulted in seventy-four enemy deaths. A captured North Vietnamese lieutenant reported that the CS had caused his troops to leave their positions, resulting in increased casualties.

According to field observation and prisoner interrogations, the discipline of the Viet Cong and the North Vietnamese Army (VC/NVA) is improving as the troops become more familiar with CS and U.S. tactics for using it. Experienced soldiers, having learned that CS is often used in coordination with artillery or air strikes or infantry assault, may choose to remain in protected positions—even though nearly incapacitated. This may or may not be a safer course of action than exposed flight, depending upon the attacker's plan. It probably is safer if the attacker intends only an antipersonnel strike. If the CS attack is followed by an infantry assault, however, the defenders will be placed in the position of trying to defend themselves in close combat at a very low level of proficiency.

CS may also be used as a flushing agent to force the enemy out of caves and tunnels whose farthest reaches are not accessible to conventional munitions. The agent can be dispensed by means of grenades aided by a blower, if one is available. In addition, its smoke-like visibility serves to disclose hidden openings to caves and tunnels.

Among the several other applications of CS in the offensive combat role in Vietnam is the suppression of ground fire around helicopter landing zones. This is usually accomplished with one of the air-delivered weapon systems. A 4th Infantry Division soldier vividly recalled jumping off a helicopter which had landed within twenty meters of a North Vietnamese soldier armed with an AK-47, who, fortunately, had been completely incapacitated by the preparatory CS fire.

CS has been found useful in foiling the Viet Cong tactic of hugging close to U.S. positions in order to thwart support by artillery and air strikes. On occasion, U.S. units have been able to lay a curtain of CS between themselves and the enemy and then pull back quickly, putting sufficient space between the two to permit artillery and tactical air strikes to be brought in.

Defensive Combat Operations

Several concepts of defensive employment of CS have become fairly standard throughout all the divisions, for example, the use for perimeter defense of the E8 launcher, which blankets an area quickly with a dense cloud of agent.

Bulk CS1 or CS2 is used to impede the approach to, and passage through, a perimeter, and to restrict passage in the area around stockpiled supplies. In the latter case, this is often aimed at civilians rather than enemy troops, as all large camps in the vicinity of civilian centers have a problem with looting. Emplacing bulk agent in proximity to friendly troops presents some wind hazard, so some of the divisions mix the agent with waste oil, which keeps the agent from being picked up by the wind. Yet anyone walking through the mixture gets enough exposure to CS to be made very uncomfortable.

Just as CS can be used to place distance between two close-in forces to permit artillery and tactical air support, so can it also be used in support of withdrawal operations to enable a smaller force to break contact with a superior force. CS grenades are regularly carried by some long-range patrols especially to facilitate such action.

As a defensive counterpart to landing-zone preparation, CS is also used to cover removal of troops by helicopter. In this case the CS cover is usually supplied by one or two helicopters performing the fire-suppression mission, employing a combination of machine gun fire, rockets, and air-delivered CS.

CS has also been used in a counter-ambush role on vehicular convoys. Several divisions have fitted various kinds of vehicles with side-mounted CS launchers. These are spaced at intervals throughout the convoy, and set to be command detonated (electrically) if the convoy is ambushed.

Reconnaissance by fire, using CS rather than conventional ordnance, has become a recognized tactic. The CS is particularly useful for checking heavily wooded areas, where it is likely to yield much better coverage of ambush fortifications than that provided by high explosives. CS munitions have also been used to probe the far bank of a canal before it is crossed. And since the airborne personnel detector ("people sniffer") missions are also flown by the division chemical staff, CS and the personnel detector are occasionally employed together. The 9th Division reported an incident in which the placement of CS on a spot indicated by the personnel detector resulted in flushing nine suspected Viet Cong into the arms of a waiting patrol.

One final example of the use of CS in Vietnam may be more aptly described as a vignette rather than a repeatable operational concept. It is, however, a very good example of how the men in the field use their ingenuity to employ whatever munitions they have available. In the period immediately after Tet, the Commanding General of an ARVN unit, in an attempt to curtail the Viet Cong resupply efforts, decreed that the villagers in the area would not be allowed to transport large amounts of foodstuffs at any one time. He received U.S. support in the form of gunship surveillance. Within a few days the airmen observed bicycle and scooter riders with large bags of rice slung across the backs of their vehicles. At first, a few warning shots "across their bow" succeeded in turning them around, but in very short order they were back again. This time, in addition to the rice, they carried women and children. Knowing that the Americans would not shoot to kill, they did not respond to the warning shots. However, one of the gunners had some CS grenades aboard and he dropped them in front of the bicycles, which got to the edge of the cloud and then promptly turned around. Word was rapidly circulated that an effective means had been found to thwart the transport of food by this brazen method by the enemy.

CS as a Nonlethal Weapon: Present and Potential

Any discussion of CS as a nonlethal weapon perforce draws heavily on the U.S. experience in Vietnam; it is necessary to look at the past five years for indicators of the future.

It is important to emphasize that CS is an agent with two distinct roles. On the one hand, it can be used to flush or to overcome the enemy with the aim of rendering him more susceptible to conventional lethal weapons (small arms, artillery, air strikes); and on the other hand, it can combine military effectiveness with the possibility of a nonlethal final consequence to enemy soldiers and, more importantly, to nearby noncombatants.

Large-scale use of riot control agents was originally publicly justified largely on the basis of minimizing civilian casualties. While this is still a popular conception of the use of CS, in actuality it seldom has been used in Vietnam with this as the primary goal. It is difficult to find specific incidents where CS was used primarily because of its nonlethal character. One instance, in fact, was described in 1968 as ". . . the only known employment of CS in such a manner in the Nth division area of operation." It occurred during Tet when an enemy force closed on an ARVN compound in the vicinity of New Plei Do Lim (Pleiku Province), herding a large group of Montagnards mixed with their own troops. As the enemy neared the compound, the ARVN defenders threw a number of CS grenades upwind of the attackers. When the agent reached them, the civilians panicked, some dropping to the ground, some ignoring the Viet Cong and running away. The enemy, deprived of civilian cover, turned and fled.

While other examples could be cited, CS is rather infrequently used only to spare civilian lives. One is led to wonder why. The answer is somewhat surprising in view of the considerable number of civilian casualties the war has produced. It appears that CS is rarely used against mixed groups of enemy and noncombatants because such groups are rarely encountered. Despite all the discussion of the Viet Cong and North Vietnamese soldiers invading a friendly or neutral village and then battling to hold it, one thing is clear: before the battle develops, the villagers remove themselve from the battlefield. On this point, the troops in the field are unanimous and adamant. Civilians hardly ever become embroiled in a firefight unless it develops very suddenly—and that is not a common occurrence. When the Viet Cong set up fighting positions in or around a village, they may force the villagers to help dig trenchworks, but they almost always permit the civilians to leave once the work is finished. The result is that before the battle begins the villagers are gone. As a matter of fact, it is well known among U.S. troops in Vietnam that one of the surest indicators that a patrol approaching a village can have of impending trouble is the absence of villagers from view.

The first problem in analyzing whether CS could be more effectively used to spare noncombatants is to determine how civilian lives are lost, and subsequently, to examine the possibility that CS could in some way affect these situations. The details behind the bare casualty figures are very difficult to uncover. However, from discussions with experienced officers and troops in the field, from on-the-spot reports, and from certain news accounts, some indicators of the principal casualty sources emerge.

Certainly some significant fraction must be laid at the doorstep of the Viet Cong and North Vietnamese. Their use of mines on heavily traveled roads, of explosives planted in public places, and of mortars and rockets against nonmilitary targets is part of a calculated campaign to terrorize and coerce the civilian populace of South Vietnam.

By contrast, injuries to civilians caused by U.S. and South Vietnamese forces are usually unsystematic and unpremeditated. They arise from a variety of causes. One is simply mistaken identification—for example, air or artillery attacks on individuals mistakenly thought to be enemy soldiers. Targeting error is another. Into this category falls the rare, but very damaging, bombing of a village incorrectly designated as enemy. A third cause might be labeled errors of judgment, as when aircraft are drawn into an attack upon a village by enemy fire intended to provoke just such a response. Also there are cases in which civilians either enter or fail to evacuate a "free fire" zone, knowingly or not, and fall victim to artillery fire or air strikes.

In addition to these examples, there are also instances in which heavy ordnance, such as artillery and bombs, although aimed at proper targets, strike wide of the mark by a significant margin. Given the existing imprecision of air-delivered ordnance and a preponderance of unobserved artillery fire, casualties have undoubtedly resulted when civilians have not moved sufficiently far away from what they have judged to be the battle area. Moreover, while they would be reasonably safe from small-arms fire in below-ground shelters—even uncovered ones—this would not necessarily be the case if they were subjected to bombing and shelling.

In sum, it appears that a large proportion of the civilian casualties caused by U.S. and South Vietnamese forces result from bombs and large ordnance rather than small-arms fire. If this is truly the case, then greater use of CS is not likely to have a significant effect on the civilian casualty rate, since it is hardly conceivable that CS could very often serve to replace large high explosive ordnance. Nevertheless, it is worth noting that the record does show a number of occasions when such ordnance was foresworn in favor of CS because of the proximity of noncombatants to enemy forces. It is simply a matter of placing these opportunities in perspective by pointing out that they do not arise very often.

There is one paradox in the use of CS around civilians that must be noted. Over the years a bomb shelter—a dugout in the floor, sometimes covered—has become a standard appurtenance of dwellings in Vietnam. If a villager does not have sufficient time to flee when he believes a battle is going to develop, he and his family may take refuge in this shelter. There is the possibility then that the use of CS in the village may have the effect of driving the villagers out of their relatively safe positions, and as they attempt to flee the cloud, increase their vulnerability to air strikes and to artillery and small-arms fire.

The Potential of CS for Minimizing Destruction

In addition to a potential for reducing civilian casualties, non-lethal chemical agents may also have potential value for reducing destruction to civilian housing and facilities during combat in built-up areas. Again, the experience of its use in Vietnam is instructive. A number of Vietnamese cities (Hue, Ban Me Thuot, My Tho, Kontum, and Cholon, for example) sustained major damage during the Tet fighting; by the end of the counter-offensive, they presented excellent, if doleful, examples of the effects of large-scale application of artillery and bombs in an urban setting.

In Hue, Kontum, and Cholon, CS was used by U.S. and ARVN forces—and to good effect. But again, it was nearly always used for its military value, not for its nonlethal/nondestructive quality.

Although CS munitions have not in the past been used very often to save lives and limit destruction, it is pertinent to ask to what degree CS munitions might be substituted for high explosives in urban warfare. The point of departure in this calculation must be the assumption that the enemy is not equipped with proper gas masks; if he is, CS will be of little value. Even against an unmasked enemy, the choice of CS in place of high explosives will often be equivocal, since a dead or seriously wounded enemy is far less dangerous than an enemy temporarily incapacitated. Thus, the commander on the scene must weigh the virtue of diminishing property damage against the very real possibility that he is increasing the danger to his own men. Psychologically, it is bound to be very difficult to avoid tipping the scale heavily in favor of minimizing the risk to his own personnel. Dealing with a situation in which civilians are endangered, it is not at all improbable that a soldier will accept a heightened risk to himself to reduce the risk to these noncombatants. Conceivably, national leadership could also ask a soldier to accept heightened personal risk in favor of minimizing damage to some specially treasured edifice. But what can be asked of a man facing a complex of strong-points set up by the enemy in a row of very ordinary apartment buildings? To the soldier engaged in a fight for his life, a huge explosion on the enemy position is a truly satisfying spectacle. Telling that man that, out of humanitarian and political considerations, he must forgo support by explosive ordnance and rush the position with CS and small arms could create a considerable morale problem.

It is difficult to provide a satisfactory answer to the question whether or not riot control agents have a largely untapped potential for curtailing the destructiveness of urban warfare. It is likely that there is no pat, blanket answer, but rather that each situation will have to be assessed individually. From the experience in Vietnam, it appears that although there are some occasions when CS *can* serve this purpose, there are also a great many when it cannot.

Reaction of the Viet Cong and the North Vietnamese to the Use of Riot Control Agents

Lessons in the utility of riot control agents in warfare have not been lost on the enemy. Because of a very limited supply situation, the VC/NVA do not use CS very often. But they certainly do use it, and to good effect, when they can. On 16 February 1968, Vietnamese marines fighting in the north-east corner of the Hue Citadel were hit by eight enemy CS mortar rounds. And as recently as March 1970, a group of NVA soldiers defending the Black Virgin Mountain near Tay Ninh covered their retreat with a large quantity of gas.

The VC/NVA supply of CS munitions is thought to come mostly from captured U.S. and ARVN stock. They have U.S. grenades; in addition, it is well known that they collect bulk agent from dud barrel bombs and then use it to fill crude grenades in the field. Sixty-millimeter and 82-millimeter mortar shells have been found in which CS1 in glass vials has been substituted for a part of the high explosive charge. The enemy may also have been supplied with some Communist Chinese CS grenades although this has not yet been verified.

The defensive capability of the VC/NVA presents a mixed picture. Their defensive masks range all the way from the Soviet Shlem mask to instructions on how to cope with CS by using a cloth soaked in lemon juice or a bit of charcoal placed in the nostrils. The Shlem is a very good all-purpose mask but, being of the hood type, is probably even more uncomfortable in the tropical climate of Vietnam than our own M-17. The Soviet Shlem is not being supplied to the NVA in any great numbers, and with a few exceptions, is limited to NVA regulars in the northern half of the country.

The Chinese two-piece mask is a more common item of issue. U.S. tests have shown that this mask has several design and quality defects, and offers only fair protection against CS.

Finally, the most common protective device carried by the Viet Cong field forces is a field-expedient mask manufactured from light plastic of the type used for raincoats in Vietnam. A piece of clear plastic is sewn in for vision, and several layers of gauze and cotton, or part of a sanitary napkin, are sewn in for air filtration. Sometimes a bit of charcoal is placed between the layers of the filter. The mask is designed either as a full hood or as a face covering only. In either case, it affords only a minimal degree of protection.

Conclusions on Military Usefulness

CS agent has found considerable acceptance in Vietnam as a

military weapon useful in certain situations. There is no doubt that it has, from time to time, also spared civilian lives and, to a lesser extent, property. One of the major obstacles, however, to an accurate assessment of the value of CS to the whole effort in Vietnam is the lack of quantifiable yardsticks of effectiveness. Instead of measures of value, only anecdotes can be found. No one has any idea of how many lives CS saves, or how many it fails to save. Moreover, since CS is primarily used to deny base camps, tunnels, caves, and terrain points, there probably is no solid measure of effectiveness; one can only presume that these actions contribute some unknown quantity to the cumulative pressure that is maintained against the enemy's forces. While some components of this problem could be researched on a roughly quantitative basis, for the time being it is not known how effective CS has been in the overall context of the war. In a sense, the case of CS reflects in microcosm one of the greatly unsatisfying aspects of the Vietnam war itself: an inability to discover a reliable means for measuring success and failure.

It is important, however, that the value of anecdotes not be dismissed lightly, if only because of the unmistakable trend they demonstrate. The great preponderance of a sample of U.S. troops interviewed in the field in 1968 (who had been in operations in which CS was used) responded with some enthusiasm. Only a few believed it did not contribute to their combat capability. However, by 1970 there were indications that the troops were less enthusiastic about the value of CS, possibly because of changes in the nature of the war and the tactics of the enemy. Still, these observations, although unquantified, must be construed to support the conclusion that CS possesses significant military worth, at least in certain situations that have occurred in the Vietnam war.

One measure of the effectiveness of a weapon, especially when it comprises, as does CS, a distinct class of weapons, is the enemy's response to it, that is, the effort he makes to counter it. In this case, the VC/NVA face two problems, one easily soluble, the other not.

The difficult problem is coping with base camps, bunkers, and tunnels that have been treated with persistent CS. Since personnel cannot function very well for protracted periods while wearing a gas mask, it seems that they are forced to accept denial of the terrain or facility. This is what they do.

The other VC/NVA problem is coping with CS in direct engagement with allied forces. This can be accomplished with a good gas mask, many of which are available on the open market in the international arms trade. Yet the VC/NVA do not seem to have expended any great effort in this direction. It is not known why, but one plausible explanation could be that they are not sufficiently bothered by use of the agent to feel compelled either to spend money on masks in lieu of some other materiel or to burden their troops with them. This, of course, does not square with the impression of U.S. troops who feel that they use CS to good effect against the enemy.

Discussion, so far, has been focused exclusively on Vietnam in describing and evaluating the military utility of CS because it comprises the only U.S. experience with CS as a weapon. It must be borne in mind, however, that Vietnam is not typical of most wars, nor can it be considered the only model for the future. In Vietnam, the United States has faced an enemy far less well equipped to face and employ gas, and in this context, CS weapons have proven useful. Against an enemy better prepared to fight a chemical war, even one restricted to nonlethal chemicals, the value of CS to either side plummets drastically. The effect in a parity situation is likely to be a relatively even-handed addition to the hardships and complexities of life for the troops on both sides. As the United States continues to use CS and to provide CS weapons to its combat forces, it causes other nations' military forces to examine their defenses. This will stimulate the procurement of gas masks and gas weapons. Consequently, fewer adversaries will remain unprotected and unable to retaliate and the utility of CS to the United States will decrease proportionately. Fear of escalation to lethal weapons might deter the use of CS by the United States in such a situation.

In summary, in certain situations CS is a useful adjunct to other weapons. However, given the wide variety and enormous power of other available weapons and taking account of the various possible enemy responses, CS should not be expected to play a major role in determining the course of future wars in which the United States may become involved. Still, this in itself is no reason to renounce the weapon. Rather it provides background for an inquiry into the possible arms control and political benefits of doing so.

Factors Acting to Restrain Proliferation and Use of CB Weapons

Vietnam marks the first time since World War I that U.S. forces have employed gas weapons of any kind in war. Aside from the obscure gas campaign waged by Japan in Manchuria, Mussolini's generally condemned use of gas against Ethiopia, and the United Arab Republic's employment of chemicals against the Yemeni Royalists, it is the first extensive use of chemical weapons by any nation in forty-five years.

Several factors have operated to discourage nations from initiating chemical warfare and from making extensive preparations for waging it.[8] Public opinion has regarded chemical warfare as particularly uncivilized and repugnant, an attitude that has also been held by not a few political and militiary leaders. At the top levels of military planning, chemical weapons have enjoyed little attention or support in comparison with other types of weapons. To be sure, this disinterest has not been shared by chemical officers, but they have usually been shunted aside from key decision-making bodies. In comparison with the main-line military branches and services, chemical warfare services have afforded poor career opportunities for the most talented and dynamic officers.

In the past, disinterest and disuse have kept most, if not all, armies unprepared to use chemical weapons. Even where the weapons have been procured and stockpiled, they have been poorly integrated into combat forces and war plans. A few nations which possess chemical weapons have tended to regard them much more as a deterrent against the initiation of chemical warfare by the enemy than as dependable war-fighting weapons. Fear of retaliation and escalation, with unpredictable consequences, reduces the incentive to initiate chemical warfare when the opportunity occurs. Unpopularity and unfamiliarity, causing lack of preparedness or planning, have tended to keep such opportunities from occurring and from being seriously considered. Thus, psychological aversion, military disinterest, and fear of retaliation have acted and interacted to prevent chemical warfare. (In the same category and in many ways not clearly distinguished is the use of germs in war—biological warfare.) The traditional restraints against chemical—and biological—warfare are embodied in one of the oldest arms control treaties now in force, the Geneva Protocol of 1925. Its prohibition of CBW under international law adds to the moral and political forces of restraint. In addition, the Protocol places gas and germs in a distinct category, offering an explicit standard upon which nations can base their conduct.

U.S. Interest in Preventing the Proliferation of CB Weapons

In the context of both tactical and strategic war, it is very much in U.S. interest to preserve and strengthen the restraints that prevent chemical warfare and the proliferation of chemical weapons. Today, "limited" wars are fought with conventional weapons which individually have limited area effect. Although such wars can be exceedingly destructive, they become so only when great quantities of weapons are used. The wealth of the United States allows it to expend enormous quantities of conventional munitions in tactical combat. Very few countries even approach this capability. However, the proliferation of lethal chemical weapons would greatly enhance the destructive and disruptive capability of smaller and less wealthy nations. This is because these weapons have the potential of large area coverage at relatively low cost. Many of the types of munitions used in limited war could be filled with lethal chemicals. In that case, the "kill area" of light weight munitions such as mortar shells and rockets would be increased by a large factor. Even though troops can be provided with protective masks and suits, such weapons would be devastating to military units caught off guard and to the civilian population. In many situations lethal chemical weapons would favor guerrilla forces. Such forces generally have no shortage of targets. They know the locations of military installations such as base camps and support facilities. Their problem is their great inferiority in fire power. For anti-guerrilla forces, the reverse is usually true, their main tactical problem being location of the enemy. In this situation, any major enhancement of the area coverage of light weight weapons disproportionately favors less sophisticated forces operating in smaller units and capable of dispersing or mingling with the civilian population. Moreover, the proliferation of lethal chemical weapons would create greatly expanded opportunities for terror attacks on urban centers by small groups of men firing chemical rockets or mortars from the outskirts. Thus, the proliferation of chemical weapons would seriously reduce the military advantage that great wealth confers, while at the same time threatening a major increase in the violence of war and its toll among civilians.

At the strategic level, the hazard of proliferation of lethal gas weapons is also serious. Countries not possessing nuclear weapons might well be tempted to acquire a population-killing capability based on nerve gas. Under suitably chosen meteorological conditions, a small bomber force could deliver enough nerve agent to kill a large proportion of persons in a major city. Although it is unlikely that a poor nation could successfully deliver chemicals over a wide area of a country with modern air defenses, a surprise attack on one or a few coastal cities would be difficult to defend against.

Further, it should be noted that analysis and planning for the use of chemical weapons is likely to stimulate interest in the strategic possibilities of biological weapons and that the economics of anti-personnel and anti-crop biological weapons for threat or deterrence may seem particularly attractive to less wealthy nations.

To summarize, the proliferation of lethal chemical weapons would risk a major increase in the level of death and devastation in wars of all kinds. Proliferation would provide forces less wealthy and sophisticated than the United States with greatly enhanced capability for threat, harassment, and destruction. The acquisition of chemical weapons would stimulate interest in biological weapons, for the barriers against both are intertwined. The overriding objective of the United States in this area of policy should be to prevent the proliferation of chemical and biological weapons and to strengthen the barriers against their use.

Riot-Control Agents and Proliferation

The example of the world's most modern army deploying a whole panoply of newly developed gas munitions (even though labeled euphemistically "riot control munitions") cannot help but stimulate interest in the military establishments of other nations in the utility of similar weapons. It seems almost inevitable that analysis and planning for chemical warfare will increase on a worldwide basis unless an effective plan to abort such interest is developed.

Furthermore, the danger of a shift in interest from nonlethal to lethal chemical weapons is very real. The procurement of gas masks and the commencement of chemical training, which many nations might well feel forced to undertake if CS comes into general military use, would offset a considerable part of the cost of obtaining an offensive lethal chemical capability. As more military forces become accustomed to training in a chemical environment and as chemical cadres are upgraded and careers become dependent on an important role for gas, the next step leading to acquisition of lethal chemicals becomes smaller and harder to resist. Many of the techniques for the dispersal of riot control agents are similar to those employed for lethal chemicals, so that the procurement of an offensive lethal capability would be facilitated. The rapid expansion of the scale of use of CS once it was introduced in Vietnam is a good example of how a limited capability can be readily enlarged once the political barriers to the use of chemicals have been breached. Tactics are quickly developed for their use in a variety of military situations far beyond those originally envisaged.

The use of harassing gas in war provides experience and

establishes defensive preparations and logistic arrangements that can facilitate the transition to other, more toxic, gases. Once the enemy has acquired gas masks, CS and similar harassing agents lose most of their effectiveness. An obvious response in that case would be to employ skin irritants. The move to even more effective skin irritants such as mustard may not seem as great as the step of introducing harassing agents in the first place. Another source of pressure to move upward in the scale of toxic weapons could be born of desperation to retrieve a deteriorating battlefield situation where defeat would have serious political repercussions. If the use of a certain chemical weapon appeared to offer relief, political leadership might accept that onus in order to stave off worse difficulties. This decision might be much easier once the use of harassing agents had been generally accepted. It should be pointed out that even if both sides in a conflict tacitly agree to limit themselves to nonlethal agents, there may be serious difficulty in finding a mutually agreeable and workable standard, particularly as more agents with novel effects become available.

Since in some circumstances chemical weapons possess much greater persistency and area coverage capability than an equivalent weight of conventional weapons, nations not now militarily significant may be tempted to acquire chemical weapons in an attempt to raise their military strength in a single jump. Large industrial nations might be willing to supply such weapons to their smaller allies and to dissident forces that begin to see the possibilities for retaliation, threat, and harassment. Once these nations become accustomed to using riot control agents, they may be less inhibited than the United States in progressing on to lethal chemicals. The experience in Yemen, where tear gas is reported to have been the first agent employed, appears to be an example of such escalation, which occurred even though the United Arab Republic was a party to the Geneva Protocol. Indeed, the use of tear gas apparently preceded the escalation to lethal agents in every case where lethal agents have been used—in Manchuria, in Ethiopia, and in Europe during World War I.[9]

It should also be noted that the decision to employ a previously unused weapon can be preconditioned by earlier procurement practices. The large-scale use of CS in Vietnam in 1966 and since may have been made substantially more difficult to avert by the U.S. Army's purchase of 367,000 pounds of CS for Southeast Asia in fiscal 1964, almost two years before it had been generally approved for uses other than riot control. If proliferation of lethal gas weaponry occurs, political leaders may find it difficult to hold to a "no first use" policy, if there is any military pressure to use gas. This may be particularly true as the boundary line between riot control agents and lethal agents becomes blurred. The force of public opinion supporting conformance with international law, as exemplified by the Geneva Protocol, will be weakened.

The extensive use of riot control agents has had a serious effect on the U.S. ability to take international action to discourage lethal chemical warfare. When it was confirmed that numerous gas attacks had been made against the royalist side in the Yemen civil war, the United States made no move to bring public pressure against the apparent attacker, the United Arab Republic. Although there were certainly other factors involved, the use of chemicals in Vietnam was a potent influence in inhibiting the United States from urging in the United Nations a strong stand against such use. Despite President Nixon's strong, unilateral decision to forgo the use of biological warfare and most chemical warfare, the use of riot control agents in Vietnam has hindered the United States in assuming a role of world leadership in controlling CBW. Instead the United States is continually forced to adopt a defensive posture in world forums.

During the past year the Conference of the Committee on Disarmament (CCD) at Geneva has paid increasing attention to methods of controlling chemical and biological warfare.[10] The Soviet bloc has introduced a treaty that would ban the use, production, and stockpiling of both chemical and biological weapons. This has presented the United States with a difficult problem, since most nations involved believe that harassing chemical agents would be included in the category of chemical weapons. The United States has made clear that it does not agree with this definition. Probably in part because it recognized the problems which the control of chemical warfare presented the United States while it was using CS in Vietnam, the United Kingdom has put forth a draft treaty that deals only with biological warfare. While the United States and the United Kingdom are behind this proposal, many others are in favor of the more inclusive Soviet approach. Thus, instead of providing leadership in attempting to achieve President Nixon's stated objectives of eliminating both chemical and biological warfare, the United States has given the appearance of dragging its feet.

Finally, the use of riot control agents has presented the United States with serious problems in connection with the Geneva Protocol.[11] In December 1969, the United Nations General Assembly held, by a vote of 80 to 3, with 36 abstentions, that the Protocol prohibits the use in war of all toxic chemicals, without exception. In view of this, there is no likelihood in the foreseeable future of getting widespread agreement to exempt CS. On the other hand, if the United States were to relinquish the use of harassing agents in warfare, it would almost certainly obtain general agreement on the applicability of the Protocol to all anti-personnel chemicals.

The United Kingdom, under the pressure resulting from its use of CS in Northern Ireland, recently changed its position to the view that CS, but surprisingly not other riot control agents such as CN, is not included in the Protocol. However, the Cabinet was seriously divided and most of the numerous ensuing commentaries in the British press were unfavorable. Therefore the United Kingdom, particularly with a new government in charge, may well be willing to accept a uniform standard if it is reemphasized that the Protocol in no way restricts the domestic use of riot control agents for preserving order. This distinction between use in warfare and in riot control has been understood and practiced by many nations since the Protocol came into being. During World War II, United States military police were well supplied with tear gas grenades and used them on soldiers and on allied civilians in certain circumstances to quell disturbances. However, these munitions were not employed in combat against the enemy. Riot control chemicals are used for civil purposes in France, but the French government has held their use in war to be prohibited and their military manuals state this. There are many similar examples. Even Sweden, a nation that is very energetically promoting international action against the use of tear gas in war, uses CS for maintaining domestic order. Indeed, a possible threat to the freedom of police to use tear gas in the democratic countries probably comes from the risk that it will be misused in war and cause serious injury or that its massive and undisciplined employment will lead to reaction against it. These consequences can be made more, not less, likely by habituation to the large-scale use of CS in war and by the gradual transition of its image from a police aid to a war weapon.

The Geneva Protocol is an important factor in maintaining the expectation that gas will not be used. This, in turn, dampens interest and pressure for chemical weapons in many countries, especially ones where funds and facilities for military programs are sharply limited. Thus, the Protocol helps to avert proliferation of chemical weapons, benefiting the United States at least as much as any other country. Beyond that, the Protocol can provide a clear standard upon which belligerents can base their conduct in war. Creating dissension regarding the interpretation of the Protocol weakens its psychological effectiveness and calls attention to gas weapons. Furthermore, it reduces the effectiveness of the Protocol as a clear standard for agreement during war. When the simplest focus for agreement is "no gas," much of the benefit of the Protocol is lost by attempting to create exceptions.

Summary and Conclusions

President Nixon in November 1969 made it clear that the basic objective of U.S. chemical-biological warfare policy was to eliminate these forms of weapons from the arsenals of the world. Nevertheless, riot control or harassing chemical agents have in the last few years found considerable utility as normal military weapons in the conflict in Vietnam, where logistical problems complicate the ability of the enemy to provide its forces with gas masks. Riot control agents also provide the potential for reducing civilian casualties in situations where military and civilians are intermingled, although this has not occurred nearly as frequently in Vietnam as originally anticipated. On the other hand, the use of harassing agents for military purposes erodes the fire break between conventional weapons and so-called weapons of mass destruction. It increases the likelihood that other nations will not only use these weapons but more lethal ones as well. Such worldwide use not only is contrary to the President's basic political objective of banning CBW, but also could lead in the long run to decreased U.S. security.

The key issue that must be faced by U.S. policy-makers is whether the military gain from continuing use of riot control agents in military operations in Vietnam overrides the longer-range harm that such use may cause our basic CBW policy. As the United States continues to use CS, the forces of opposing nations will develop defensive tactics and will seek to acquire gas masks and gas weapons of their own. As a result, the military utility of CS to U.S. forces will decline. In contrast, U.S. interest in averting the proliferation of chemical weapons will continue and intensify with the capability of progressively more countries to produce weapons once considered the monopoly of the most advanced nations, and as future discoveries in chemistry and biology open up new avenues for possible military exploitation. If the long-term disadvantages are deemed sufficiently serious, then means must be devised for halting the use of these agents in Vietnam in such a manner as to minimize the danger to U.S. military operations. It is the authors' view that the limited military value of CS in Vietnam, the gradual decrease in U.S. involvement in Vietnam, and the need for the United States to provide leadership in eliminating CBW all dictate a U.S. policy that would lead to the phasing out of the use of riot control agents and to a return to the traditional U.S. stance of not using gas weapons of any kind in war.

REFERENCES

1. See pp. 4, 8–14.
2. The conceptual distinction between "lethal" and "nonlethal" chemical agents requires some explanation. No agent, and certainly not one intended to produce an irritating physiological reaction, is nonlethal in absolute terms. For military purposes, a nonlethal agent is one which has a sufficiently wide spread between its effective dose (the dose at which it elicits the desired symptom) and its minimum lethal dose as to permit it to be employed in a given situation with only a very slight lethal danger to the target population. As an example, the lethal toxicity of chlorine, which was successfully employed as a lethal agent in World War I, is not much different from that of the nonlethal agents CN, CS, and DM. The difference is that the latter agents are significantly harassing at airborne concentrations approximately one hundred times smaller than chlorine. It should be pointed out that both effective dose and lethal dose vary from one recipient to the next. Thus, it is possible that a dose of a given agent that is merely harassing for a reasonably healthy adult might be sufficient to aggravate a serious preexisting condition in another person, or pose a threat to the very young or aged. The best nonlethal agents minimize these complications by virtue of their large safety factors (i.e., the spread between effective dose and lethal dose).
3. A. A. Fries and C. J. West, *Chemical Warfare* (New York: McGraw Hill, 1921), pp. 15–16.
4. Albert Speer, *Inside the Third Reich* (New York: Macmillan, 1970), pp. 489–490.
5. U.S. Department of State *Bulletin,* Vol. LII, No. 1346 (12 Apr. 1965), pp. 529, 531.
6. The specific examples in this section of the use of CS in military operations in Vietnam were supplied informally by the U.S. Army.
7. U.S. Dept. of the Army, Training Circular TC 3–16, Apr. 1969.
8. For a detailed analysis of the restraints against chemical warfare, see Maj. Frederic J. Brown, *Chemical Warfare, A Study in Restraints* (Princeton, N. J.: Princeton Univ. Press, 1968).
9. See Stockholm International Peace Research Institute, *The Problem of Chemical and Biological Warfare* (Provisional ed., 1970), Part I: History.
10. See pp. 97–108.
11. See pp. 2–14.

LIMITATIONS ON CHEMICAL AND BIOLOGICAL WARFARE GOING BEYOND THOSE OF THE GENEVA PROTOCOL

by Archibald S. Alexander

Chemical warfare (CW) occupies a special position of distaste in the public consciousness, originating during World
War I. This distaste was shown also for biological warfare
(BW) in the terms of the Geneva Protocol of 1925 and in
proposals for other treaties. It is renewed whenever the use
of CBW weapons is proven or even charged. It should prove
to be of psychological help in achieving further arms limitations in the field of CBW.

The feelings of distaste have lately been further reinforced
as the public has become aware that the use of CBW agents
may have secondary effects, some unpredictable, which may
have serious consequences on man, animals, and the environment. As it was put in the conclusion of the unanimous report
submitted on 30 June 1969 to the Secretary-General of the
United Nations by consultant experts:

> Were these weapons ever to be used on a large scale in war,
> no one could predict how enduring the effects would be and
> how they would affect the structure of society and the environ-
> ment in which we live. This overriding danger would apply as
> much to the country which initiated the use of these weapons
> as to the one which had been attacked, regardless of what
> protective measures it might have taken in parallel with its
> development of an offensive capability. A particular danger
> also derives from the fact that any country could develop or
> acquire, in one way or another, a capability in this type of
> warfare, despite the fact that this could prove costly. The
> danger of the proliferation of this class of weapons applies as
> much to the developing as it does to developed countries.[1]

Note: This article deals with various means of controlling chemical
and biological warfare (CBW), over and above the effect of
United States ratification of the Geneva Protocol. It assumes that
domestic use of tear gas and pesticides will continue to be permitted.

A similar feeling of revulsion against CBW was reflected in Resolution 2603 A (XXIV) of the United Nations General Assembly, adopted on 16 December 1969 (80 for, 3 against, 36 abstentions). This resolution, against which the United States voted, declared the use in warfare of any chemical or biological agent to be contrary to the "generally recognized rules of international law." The resolution clearly was intended to apply to riot control agents or defoliants as well as to lethal or incapacitating agents.

The subject will be considered in three parts:

I. The need to secure the adherence to the Geneva Protocol of the other countries not now parties whose failure to be bound might endanger the effectiveness of the Protocol.

II. Measures on biological warfare going beyond the Geneva Protocol.

III. Measures on chemical warfare going beyond the Geneva Protocol.

The Need To Secure the Adherence to the Geneva Protocol of the Other Countries Not Now Parties Whose Failure To Be Bound Might Endanger the Effectiveness of the Protocol

It is desirable to make the prohibitions of the Geneva Protocol, limiting both biological and chemical warfare, as effective as possible by securing universal adherence. Otherwise there are loopholes for use of CBW weapons—for instance in retaliation—which are likely to result in general escalation to more and more destructive weapons. Many countries have adhered to the Protocol on the basis that they are not precluded from retaliation, at least in measured or equivalent terms, and that they are bound by the terms of the Protocol only as to countries that have adhered to it. The possibility of removing these limitations on the ban imposed by the Protocol should be borne in mind. This will be considered later in this article. Meanwhile, however, every effort ought to be made to obtain further adherence.

The countries that have not adhered to the Protocol to date may be divided into three categories: countries with the industrial base, the technical skill, and the military machinery that make them actual or potential major CBW powers; countries capable of mounting small-scale efforts that could threaten other smaller powers or that might permit limited or sneak attacks against larger countries; and the others, which are potential CBW victims without having a serious CBW capability themselves.

As to the first two categories, it is clearly important to bring all such countries into the fold. So long as a potential CBW power is not bound by treaty, there is a greater risk that it may be tempted to use CBW agents in war; and this risk will tend to induce concern, stockpiling of CBW weapons, and preemptive or other use by other powers having CBW weapons.

Despite the possibility that international law or a prudent respect for the opinion of mankind might protect one of the smaller powers from attack by a CBW power, it would seem to be in the clear interest of the smaller powers to secure the benefits of the Protocol. This would increase the inhibitions of the major powers as to use against smaller powers.

Furthermore, the possibility of use by a small power allied to a great power should be eliminated. This possibility has serious implications because of the reservations made by many countries adhering to the Protocol, releasing the adherent as to an enemy if either the enemy or its allies fail to respect the prohibitions of the Protocol. Thus, if major powers A and B have adhered to the Protocol, A would be released from its obligation not to initiate CBW against B if B's ally, small power N, should use CBW against A. Even in the absence of general hostilities, if a member of NATO or the Warsaw Pact alliance were involved, there would be the risk of spread of use of CBW weapons without violation of international treaty obligations.

Of the countries in addition to the United States that are not parties to the Protocol (as of mid-1970), some are specially significant, and their early adherence would be desirable. Some of these are Brazil, Colombia, Ecuador, and Peru in South America; all the Central American countries except Mexico; Jordan, Saudi Arabia, and Yemen in the Middle East; and a number of African countries, including Algeria, Morocco, and several other Francophone countries, such as Ivory Coast. A number of these countries have cast anti-CBW votes in the United Nations General Assembly. In the Far East, the ratification by Japan in May 1970 is a very favorable development which should help persuade other countries not yet parties.

Of the major powers—including the NATO and Warsaw Pact members, Japan, and Mainland China—only the United States has not yet ratified the Geneva Protocol. It is important that the United States act promptly to complete action on President Nixon's commitment in his statement of 25 November 1969: "the Administration will submit to the Senate, for its advice and consent to ratification, the Geneva Protocol of 1925." If there is further delay, the United States may lose the opportunity to achieve universal ratification which Japan's recent action created. Once the United States becomes a party to the Geneva Protocol, it would certainly be appropriate to put discreet diplomatic pressure on the remaining countries, in addition to the moral suasion embodied in various United Nations actions. As additional countries adhere to the Protocol, the commitment of countries that had previously done so would be psychologically renewed.

Measures on Biological Warfare Going Beyond Those of the Geneva Protocol

By the terms of President Nixon's statements of 25 November 1969 and 18 February 1970, the United States has renounced the use, "development, procurement or stockpiling of biological weapons,"[2] including toxins. United States policy on BW and the use of toxins in warfare, as indicated by the President's statements, can be outlined as follows:

1. The use of biological agents and weapons, whether lethal or not, is renounced. Since there is no exception made, use against humans, animals, or plants is precluded. The renunciation thus applies to biological anti-crop weapons, such as wheat rust, but does not cover

chemical agents like those used for defoliation and destruction of food crops.

2. Research will be confined to "defensive measures, such as immunization and safety measures."

3. Recommendations are to be made as to the disposal of existing stocks of BW weapons.

4. Toxins, which are generally produced from biological agents but are not themselves living and may therefore be deemed to be chemical agents, will be subject to the same ban as active biological agents.

It was later announced by U.S. government spokesmen that all production of BW agents had been terminated, though "very minor quantities" might have to be produced for defensive purposes, such as for immunization.

These substantial steps on the part of the United States involve not only arms control, but also disarmament. Other countries, if they have adhered to the Geneva Protocol, have bound themselves not to use "bacteriological methods of warfare . . . as between themselves." The Protocol, however, stops considerably short of the present U.S. policy in the field of BW. The Protocol deals only with the use of BW weapons, not with their development, production, or stockpiling; it only applies for the benefit of countries that have ratified it; and many countries adhered with a reservation of the right to retaliate. Additional countries, particularly if they have the technical and other capabilities for the production of BW agents, should be urged to bridge the gap by following the American example of total renunciation of use, production and stockpiling, and limitation of research to defensive measures. In addition to the United States, the Federal Republic of Germany (1954), and Austria have gone beyond the Geneva Protocol with regard to BW. The Netherlands, in ratifying the Protocol, did not reserve the right to retaliate with BW, and was probably the first country to renounce BW completely. In March 1970, Canada formally stated that "it never has and does not now possess any biological weapons (or toxins) and does not intend to develop, produce, acquire, stockpile or use such weapons at any time in the future."[3]

Further action to renounce BW could be taken by means of any one of the following: (a) international agreement; (b) deposit of unilateral declaration; (c) informal unilateral action; or (d) a United Nations resolution.

A. International Agreement

1. *British draft convention.* A revised draft convention on biological warfare was submitted by the United Kingdom to the Conference of the Eighteen Nation Committee on Disarmament (ENDC) in August 1969.[4] The method of dealing with the problem proposed in the British draft may be described by a summary of the draft.

Article I binds each party "never in any circumstances, by making use for hostile purposes" of biological agents "causing death, damage or disease by infection or infestation to man, other animals, or crops, to engage in biological methods of warfare." This prohibition of biological methods of warfare is sweeping. It apparently forbids the use of *any* biological agent, whether or not in retaliation, against *any* country, whether or not a party to the agreement. A possible gap, which could be readily eliminated by clarifying language, involves doubt whether a BW agent could legally be used in warfare against plants other than crops, for example for tree defoliation. It would also be desirable to make it clear that toxins are included in the proscribed BW agents.

Article II binds the parties "not to produce or otherwise acquire, or assist in or permit the production or acquisition of" biological agents of the type and quantity which might be used in warfare, or the equipment required to disseminate an agent. The parties are also bound by this article to refrain from research aimed at production of offensive biological agents and to "destroy, or divert to peaceful purposes, within three months" after becoming bound by the agreement, its stocks of agents or disseminators.

Means of protection against BW, and research needed to acquire them, are not banned. A difficulty arises in this connection because of the similarity, in some instances, between research for offensive purposes and research for defensive purposes. However, as to many possible BW items, no confusion would be possible, because the testing of agents by the use of weapons, or the production or stockpiling of appreciable quantities of agents, would be hard to disguise—assuming an open society or reasonable access—and hard to justify as part of a defensive program. The three month interval allowed by the British draft for destruction of stocks seems somewhat short. Also, it may be desirable to add a provision for destruction or conversion of production facilities.

Provisions for verification of elimination of stocks are not included in the British draft agreement, though Article III includes a complaint procedure described below. Verification should present little difficulty from the point of view of intrusiveness so far as declared stocks are concerned. There would be greater difficulty in case of undeclared but suspected quantities; presumably the complaint procedure could apply to this case. A difficulty may arise as to countries which, like the Soviet Union, have not admitted possession of BW weapons and may therefore not wish to declare stocks in fact held.

Article III contains the only provisions in the draft convention which deal with the verification or safeguard problem. The provisions are three-fold:

1. A party "which believes that biological methods of warfare have been used against it may lodge a complaint with the Secretary-General of the United Nations," submitting its evidence and asking that the complaint be investigated and reported on to the Security Council.
2. A party to the convention, not itself the victim of a BW attack, may, if it believes another party has violated the provisions of Articles I and II, lodge a complaint with the Security Council, submitting its evidence and asking investigation of the complaint.
3. Parties agree to cooperate "fully" with the Secretary-General and his representatives in the investigation of a complaint.

One problem presented under this article is the difficulty of proving use of biological agents because of the long incubation period sometimes involved and because of the incidence of epidemic or other manifestations of diseases that occur from natural causes, but are similar to what BW agents might cause.

As a means of helping verification as to facilities which are or might be used for producing offensive BW agents, it has been suggested that they be opened to the public and devoted to public health research or manufacture. This could be applied in the United States to the biological facilities at Pine Bluff and Fort Detrick, for example. A problem in opening up facilities so fully is that plants may be privately owned in a country like the United States. There might be reluctance on the part of companies having proprietary processes, because of the risk of disclosing information which might be of advantage to competitors. However, at the present time, plants for pharmaceutical products are open to inspection by public health authorities, from other countries as well as from the country where the plant is located. This requirement is imposed by the public health laws of countries in which the products are to be sold. It is also interesting to note that it is technically difficult to convert a commercial vaccine plant to the production of a military BW agent. Furthermore, the extreme safety precautions that must be taken at a plant manufacturing BW agents are likely to make the plant hard to conceal. Indeed, countries with a BW agent capability tend to manufacture BW products in government-owned and -operated plants rather than in commerically owned facilities or in facilities owned by the government but commercially operated.

Article III might usefully be amended to give a nation that does not have sophisticated facilities for verifying or detecting the use of BW the opportunity to obtain the help of an international group for that purpose. Such a group might be the World Health Organization, the International Committee of the Red Cross, or an arms control organization.

There is little likelihood that, given the present state of international relations, any major power will accept the foreign presence required for verification before a possible violation. However, the provisions of the British draft present an alternative to pre-violation on-site inspection. The second paragraph of Article III would permit a complaint and investigation if there were evidence acquired without on-site inspection.[5] Such a complaint could be made if there were reason to suspect the existence of either production facilities or stocks of BW agents.

Article IX provides that the convention shall be of unlimited duration, but that—as in recent international arms control agreements—each party may withdraw, "if it decides that extraordinary events, related to the subject matter of this convention, have jeopardized the supreme interests of its country."

The British draft convention as a whole represents a careful effort, in short compass, to deal with the major problems involved in eliminating BW, in a world composed of countries of many different kinds and sizes, with varying degrees of reluctance to submit to on-site verification. In his statement of 25 November 1969, President Nixon said:

> The United States associates itself with the principles and objectives of the United Kingdom draft convention, which would ban the use of biological methods of warfare. We will seek, however, to clarify specific provisions of the draft to assure that necessary safeguards are included.

Since the United States, as the President announced in the same statement, has renounced the use of all methods of BW, as well as production and stockpiling of BW weapons, and will confine its research to defensive measures, it would appear that the lack of infallible means of verification, including on-site methods, does not preclude the giving up of offensive BW agents and stocks of weapons. The President did not consider that the national security of the United States would be in jeopardy if these weapons and agents were renounced. There would be even less risk if the complaint and investigation procedures contemplated by the British draft convention were accepted by other countries.

2. *Warsaw Pact and related proposals.* The Warsaw Pact powers have proposed a convention that deals with both chemical and biological weapons. The provisions of this draft convention were outlined in a letter dated 19 September 1969 from the United Nations representatives of the Warsaw Pact

countries to the Secretary-General of the United Nations. This convention would bind each party not ''to develop, produce, stockpile or otherwise acquire'' CBW weapons, to destroy or divert to peaceful uses all such weapons in its possession, and not proliferate or help or encourage proliferation. But there is no provision for international inspection or other forms of verification, whether before the fact or afterwards. Instead, each state is "internationally responsible for compliance" within its own territory and for the compliance of its citizens or instrumentalities outside its territory.

In connection with the convention proposed by the Warsaw Pact countries, Hungary, Mongolia, and Poland on 14 April 1970, submitted a working paper to the Conference of the Committee on Disarmament (CCD).[6] These three countries suggested the inclusion in the convention of a new article containing a provision for the lodging of a complaint with the Security Council of the United Nations, similar to the procedure suggested in the British BW draft convention. In addition, the new article contains an undertaking by each party to the convention "to cooperate in carrying out any investigations which the Security Council may undertake."

In the discussion of the working paper at the CCD, the Polish representative stressed this obligation to cooperate with whatever the Security Council decides.[7] He added, "should the Security Council decide, for example, on the need for an on-site inspection then of course that inspection should be carried out." He also stated acceptance of the Swedish view that the objective of verification is to generate mutual trust, and that a complaint procedure need not insure total observance of the convention. But he pointed out that the Security Council, in accordance with the United Nations Charter, "would be in a position to take all appropriate steps resulting from the process of the investigation so that any would-be violator would have no chance of escaping sanctions." He then very frankly discussed the matter of the possible application of the veto in the Security Council. He dealt with this possibility by simply saying that there could be "theoretically a more sophisticated and effective system of security than that provided for in the Charter of the UN. But, let us face it, no better system of security has been worked out so far and we doubt whether the foreseeable future will bring changes in this respect."

A significant pronouncement on the subject of CBW was made at a CCD session on 16 April 1970 by the representative of Yugoslavia.[8] After some general remarks relating to "control[9] or verification" he reached certain conclusions.

He favored whatever would lessen "the high degree of mistrust which exists in the present-day world." Greater frankness, and therefore some kind of "control," would contribute to reducing the mistrust, he said. By the same token, because of "present international conditions," the absence of "a certain degree of control" might either prevent an arms control agreement or permit it to be followed by events which would either make the agreement unstable or result in "constant suspicions leading to other negative steps." He favored a control system that would be designed primarily to meet the following requirements:

1. It should fulfil its intent—in other words, be efficient to the point of not leaving open any possibilities for undetected violations of decisive importance.

2. It should not inflict commercial or other damage through the revealing of industrial, scientific and other secrets.

3. Its functioning should be relatively easy and simple.

4. Expenses for the control should be kept at the lowest possible level.

The Yugoslav representative expressed the view that no system could possibly offer "one hundred percent control" over all installations and institutions which could assist in research, development, production, or stockpiling of CBW weapons. But he said "we must also agree that one hundred percent control is not indispensable. . . . clandestine production and possession of such limited quantities of chemical and biological weapons as have no real military importance" would have to be considered an acceptable possibility. He then spelled out four categories of possible elements of a system of verification or control. They were:

(1) "Legal measures of renunciation and self-control adopted by each country." Examples of these would be a law placing institutions now engaged in research, development, or production in the CBW field under civilian administration or control, or a law that would prohibit research for weapons purposes and the development, production, or stockpiling of agents, along with a decision to eliminate existing stocks and test sites. Such legal measures would also include legislation prohibiting further training of the military in the use of CBW weapons.

(2) "Measures of indirect control" carried out under international auspices or by individual countries, based on official statements and on analyses of scientific and other public information.

(3) "Measures of international control." This could include the publication by governments of a list of "all institutions, factories, proving grounds and the like" engaged in CBW work before the ban. There would also be a list of institutions "which by their nature could be engaged in such activities." Governments would also be expected to provide the possibility of properly regulated access by foreign inspectors, along the lines of the verification by challenge suggested by the Swedish representative.[10] Also included would be the possibility of verification by satellites and other remote detection devices; as to these, countries would have to make public more information concerning the technologies involved and their capabilities.

(4) "A complaints procedure." This proposal is very similar to the one contained in the United Kingdom draft convention on BW. The Yugoslav representative recognized the problem of the veto, but said, "It is a separate issue which I do not intend to deal with now."

He concluded with the remark that acceptance of "control," and the degree of its intrusiveness and thoroughness, were political questions, and he expressed the view that the technical and other problems could be solved if there were political readiness to make an agreement.

The Warsaw Pact draft will undoubtedly appeal to some states because it deals with CW as well as BW. But it thereby raises difficulties.[11] Other states may find the Warsaw Pact draft unacceptable because it provides little or no procedure or machinery to verify compliance.

In short, the political situation as to further BW limitations can be summed up as follows:

(1) Some Western countries would have difficulty in accepting the Warsaw Pact draft, because of the absence of verification provisions. The Warsaw Pact countries probably realize this; the draft may be a kind of first offer, with which they have started the bargaining. Indeed, the Polish statement in the CCD represents some movement towards acceptance of on-site inspection after challenge.

(2) The British draft convention appears unacceptable to many countries because it does not deal with CW; if it were broadened to cover CW, it might be acceptable to such countries.

One possible solution to the impasse might be the acceptance by the Warsaw Pact countries of the principle of complaint and verification of violations in the manner of the British draft, while the NATO countries, and presumably the Third World, would accede to coverage of CW in addition to BW.

B. *Deposit of Unilateral Declaration*

If a treaty going beyond the Geneva Protocol appears unattainable, a possible alternative approach would be to set up a procedure for the registering of appropriate renunciations of biological warfare and weapons. This would presumably take place under United Nations auspices; and a country would deposit its statement with the United Nations or with agreed depository governments to indicate its accepance of the principle of renunciation. The act of deposit would create a binding moral, if not legal, obligation. It would be preferable for the renunciations to use uniform texts. The statement would presumably contain an undertaking along the lines of one recently announced by President Nixon.

As the nations taking the lead register their renunciations, pressure would certainly build up on the remaining countries not to stand aloof, and it would be likely that members of alliances would take identical action. Failure to register might well be seen, both domestically and internationally, as a possible indication of a BW capability or the intention to acquire one.

On the other hand, a country might be unwilling to accept such a burden—one similar to that imposed by a treaty but without the advantages of a treaty. In the United States, the executive branch might not be willing to undertake—and perhaps could not do so constitutionally—this kind of obligation in lieu of a treaty without seeking the advice and consent of the Senate. There would then be a risk that the Senate might block action, as could, of course, occur with a treaty.

This procedure should be considered as an alternative only if it becomes apparent that sufficient international agreement cannot be reached on a treaty.

C. *Informal Unilateral Action*

Another possibility lies in unilateral action, similar to that taken in the decision by President Nixon, without formal deposit of any statement with an international body but containing an invitation to other countries to take similar action.

This could be a step-by-step approach to the objectives of a treaty. It would be less effective than a treaty. Legally, at least, unilateral action may be unilaterally withdrawn, whereas a treaty involves the contractual obligations of the other parties. But unilateral action, if most of the important powers take it, would be preferable to none.

D. *United Nations Resolution*

If efforts to obtain a treaty, registration, or unilateral action were unsuccessful, there would remain the possibility of seeking a resolution in the United Nations. This could only be hortatory rather than binding, but it would serve, if unanimous or nearly so, to express again the distaste of the member states for BW. It would also maintain some momentum in this field. It might pave the way for stronger action, as has occurred in other fields of disarmament, for instance in regard to the use of nuclear weapons in outer space, when a treaty followed not long after the United Nations resolution. The United Nations resolution could, of course, be combined with an invitation to states to take unilateral renunciation action and to register such action with the United Nations.

As most of the countries participating in the CCD, as well as member states of the United Nations, are anxious to see momentum maintained in the field of arms control and disarmament, it is believed that the best course of action for the United States would be to join other countries in the CCD in making any required improvements in the British draft convention, such as adding CW measures if feasible, and then to place it for adoption before the countries of the world. Such action would be a good response to the 1969 report of the Secretary-General on the subject of CBW.

Measures on Chemical Warfare Going Beyond Those of the Geneva Protocol

This paper will now consider what further steps might be useful in the CW field, beyond what is provided for in the Geneva Protocol of 1925.

The present situation may be summarized by referring to the following aspects of the chemical warfare field:

(a) Use against states not parties to the Geneva Protocol is not banned by the Protocol. It may be inhibited by international law, but it has occurred since World War II. Lethal gas was used by the United Arab Republic, a party to the Geneva Protocol, against Yemen, also a party to the Protocol through the United Kingdom. Riot control or harassing agents have been used in Vietnam. In neither case was the use retaliatory. President Nixon's declarations in 1969 and 1970 have reaffirmed the U.S. policy of "renunciation of the first use of lethal chemical weapons" and have extended the renunciation to the first use of "incapacitating chemicals" and to toxins. This applies to countries that are not parties to the Geneva Protocol, as well as to those that are. The United States has not renounced use in war of chemical harassing or riot control agents or chemical defoliants, and has used them in large amounts in Vietnam. The recent reductions in such use may indicate a less favorable view of their utility, or the pressure of public opinion.

(b) Use of CW weapons in retaliation is permitted by the reservations or interpretations made by many of the countries which have adhered to the Geneva Protocol, and this covers use against members of an alliance which may not themselves have initiated CW, if one of their allies has done so. International law does not appear to have prohibited retaliatory use. The United Nations resolution of 16 December 1969, declaring the use in warfare of chemical agents contrary to "generally recognized rules of international law," may purport to alter this conclusion, though it is ambiguous, and the General Assembly is probably not the appropriate maker or interpreter of international law.

(c) Possession and manufacture of CW weapons are not covered by the Geneva Protocol or by international law. President Nixon's 1969 and 1970 policy declarations also do not cover manufacturing and stockpiling of chemical agents, or of the means of their dissemination. Article 2 of the Warsaw Pact draft convention of 1969 provides for destruction of chemical weapons, and Article 5 provides that each party to the proposed convention will take the necessary domestic "measures to prohibit development, production and stockpiling" of chemical weapons. However, powers with significant CW capabilities have not fully taken these steps, although the Western European Union and Canada have, to varying degrees, gone a good deal of the way.

(d) Retention of facilities for manufacturing CW weapons on a standby basis is not covered by the Geneva Protocol or by international law. The United States and other major powers have not renounced the right to such retention.

(e) Research in the field of CW, whether for offensive or defensive purposes, is not covered by existing treaty or by international law, and has not been renounced by the United States or other major powers. The Warsaw Pact draft convention of 1969 appears to be directed only at "development" of weapons, and therefore presumably permits research, development, and possession of materiel for defensive purposes.

(f) Proliferation, that is, transfer between nations, of CW agents, weapons, or techniques of manufacture, is not prohibited by the Geneva Protocol or by international law, and there has often been close collaboration between members of present alliances. The Warsaw Pact draft convention of 1969 contains in Article 3 a broad prohibition of proliferation (as does the United Kingdom draft, in regard to BW).

(g) Verification of compliance with a CW ban is not now covered in the Geneva Protocol, or by other legal obligations, except to an extent for the members of the Western European Union.[12]

Against this background, some of the areas in which gaps appear will be considered.

Many countries which adhered to the Geneva Protocol did so with the reservation of the right of use of CW in retaliation. The parties to the Geneva Protocol are only bound by its terms as to other parties. This situation gives rise to risks so long as nations retain CW weapons and facilities for making them. The risks could be serious, particularly if the means of dissemination were of a kind that might make it difficult to identify the source. The possibility of covert use of chemical agents, for instance by use of aerosols released offshore by a vessel when the wind drift is landward, is real enough to have been considered in the past by various powers.

There is also the danger of the use of the forbidden agents, despite a treaty, if the tide of war is going against a country having the capability to use the agents.

Finally, in case of significant limitation and reduction of nuclear weapons, there would be increased possibility that CW agents would take higher rank as strategic or tactical weapons, and the temptation to retain them as "deterrents" would be greater. The time to deal with CW is before it has come to seem too valuable.

The most serious difficulty, in seeking to go beyond the present restrictions, is the problem of verification of compliance with the ban. So far, fully effective means for international verification without on-site inspection have not been discovered, and on-site inspection is considered unacceptably intrusive by some countries.

There is also a serious difficulty due to the involvement of the United States in Vietnam, and its use there of harassing or riot control chemical agents, and chemical defoliants. Certainly, the possibility of progress in the CW field is lessened by the U.S. position that it should be permissible to use CW weapons, provided they are not "lethal" or "incapacitating," and that harassing agents or defoliants are not incapacitating. If the United States should see no further need for CW in Vietnam,[13] either because of the reduced level of its involvement there or for other reasons, it should ratify the Geneva Protocol without reservations as to harassing agents or defoliants. In that event, the Soviet Union and its allies might be more likely to agree to the inclusion of CW in a treaty of the type proposed by the United Kingdom, including after-the-fact verification.

The basic question is whether, in the absence of *completely* effective safeguards, it is prudent and realistic to go beyond the ban of the Geneva Protocol. Essentially, this depends upon the evaluation of two risks, that of having no further ban and that of not being absolutely sure of the ability to verify compliance with a ban.

The arguments in favor of retention of a CW capability have varying applicability to the major powers, particularly those with nuclear weapons, and to smaller countries.

It is, of course, possible to argue that the maximum panoply of weapons is desirable. The types of situations that may have to be met are so varied that it is natural for a military establishment to want to have the widest possible variety of means of meeting them.

On the other hand, under current world conditions, countries like the United States and the Soviet Union may be expected to continue research on means of protection, for military and civilian personnel alike. They will probably continue to have supplies of protective material, such as gas masks, and the same may be expected to be true for other larger powers, such as the countries in Europe. Thus chemical weapons are unique in the degree to which there is a rather effective defense against their use on the battlefield. Another limitation on their utility is that in relatively close quarters the problem of wind direction or shift is a serious one for an attacker wishing to use chemical weapons.

In most of Western Europe, it would be difficult, though perhaps not impossible, to obtain a serious CW capability clandestinely in such open societies, which are becoming even more closely bound together, for example by the European Economic Community and the Western European Union (which has its own ban on CW and its own system of verification).

The considerable political disadvantage inherent in the use of chemical weapons will remain. These weapons are regarded with horror, and the reaction against a country using them would be strong. There would have to be a clear and overwhelming military advantage to overcome the drawbacks to their use. For nuclear powers, the deterrent would be the nuclear weapons, so that a CW capability would have limited utility as a deterrent. Among smaller countries lacking nuclear weapons, there is some feeling that a CW capability on their part may deter aggression, at any rate by smaller countries or those of equal strength. But for them, the realistic deterrent to invasion or attack is chiefly the nuclear power in the hands of friendly or neutral countries. This is particulary true in an area like Western Europe, where members of the NATO alliance derive their present protection against the Warsaw Pact countries, in the final analysis, from the American nuclear deterrent. Deterrence does not depend upon the ability to retaliate in kind, but upon the ability to inflict unacceptable damage by whatever means. The fear of escalation to nuclear weapons would be more likely to deter the use of CW by the Soviet Union than a Western ability to retaliate in kind with CW. Extensive use of CW would be required to obtain any significant military advantage in a conflict between the NATO and Warsaw Pact nations. This would require such quantities of munitions that they could probably not be produced and deployed clandestinely. The political consequences of initiating CW would be especially severe and the risk of escalation to nuclear weapons would be particularly high for a party to a treaty banning CW. Resort to nuclear weapons, in the event of an European conflict, would be less likely if CW were banned for both sides than if the conflict were allowed to escalate through the use of CW.

Therefore, in view of (1) the relatively low utility of CW weapons in Europe, (2) the fact that they are already banned in Europe by the Geneva Protocol except in retaliation,[14] (3) the likelihood that use of the weapons would lead to escalation, (4) the particular distaste of the people of the world for chemical weapons, (5) the risk of accidents involving civilians as well as military personnel, and (6) the burden and expense which these weapons add to the already costly and complicated military establishments, the logical conclusion is that, despite the verification problems, a total ban should be sought. This should include both production and use, whether or not in retaliation. It should apply in favor of any country, whether or not it subscribes to the ban. Several general considerations support this conclusion:

1. Defense against battlefield use of chemical weapons is particularly effective. This ability to defend against CW would be particularly useful in case, despite a ban, a country kept some limited stocks clandestinely. Means of battlefield and civil defense should not be banned.

2. The nuclear deterrent would remain, as would the conventional forces, until the general world situation permits an international order within which general and complete disarmament, or at least substantial progress in that direction, can be achieved.

3. Preparation for CW on any considerable scale would probably be difficult to conceal, particularly if countries with stockpiles of existing chemical weapons agreed to verified destruction of such stockpiles.

For the reasons given above, the temptation to violate the ban should not be very great, particularly as to smaller powers and those with open societies, in which it would be difficult to acquire or possess any substantial CW capability without the fact becoming known domestically and to other nations. As to less open societies, which restrict travel and information, particularly for foreigners, there would be some risk of undetected CW preparations, but these risks could be lessened by verification activities that are not unduly intrusive. Violations of a dangerous magnitude would not be likely to escape detection for long. As mentioned by the Canadian representative at the CCD in March 1970, there are good possibilities of detecting such violations through use of some or all of the methods of (1) administrative and budgetary inspection, (2) a search through the existing literature, (3) aerial and satellite reconnaissance, (4) remote sensors, and (5) visiting inspection teams. A meeting of technical experts should explore the full capabilities of these methods, so that it might be possible to determine what combinations of these methods might provide reasonable assurance. It would also be necessary to explore in detail the degree of intrusiveness of the methods that are not unilateral, that is, that are not dependent upon "national means" such as satellite photography and that require some international presence in the country being checked.

In connection with a CW ban, and verification measures, it would be necessary to distinguish between chemicals that have no application except in warfare and those that, though they should be banned in warfare, have other legitimate applications. Chemicals that have no civilian application should be banned completely, except for the minimum necessary for research for defensive purposes. Production or possession of more than the minimum amounts authorized would be an automatic violation of the ban. Nerve agents and mustard gas are not used commercially, and end products like nerve agents Tabun and Sarin[15] are members of this group. Intermediates in the preparation of nerve agents are useful, however, in the production of pesticides, so that it might only be the final chemical reaction that would be banned. Production of chemicals that have dual application, such as tear gas, pesticides, and some toxins, would be permitted in amounts considered normal for civilian use. Similar treatment would probably be necessary in connection with industrial production of toxic chemicals like phosgene and hydrogen cyanide.

With respect to verification of restrictions on agents having no application except for CW purposes, inspection should be easier, since no serious interference with legitimate civilian production would be required. Some countries may be reluctant to permit any inspection, and American and other private industry may also have qualms. On the latter point, arguments may be advanced to overcome such qualms.[16] The production of intermediates would require some inspection in order to determine that they are not being used to make banned CW agents rather than civilian products. Since the commercial products do not involve highly toxic chemicals, forbidden production of nerve agents should be detectable because it would involve extreme safety precautions to make a CW agent. This would therefore tend to flag violations of the ban. However, if the intermediates are used to fill "binary munitions" (where the final production of the agent occurs in the munition in the course of delivery), the safety precautions need be no greater than when these intermediates are used for pesticides. In such circumstances, accounting for the production of the materials would have to be relied on, and this would not be as good a verification procedure. Accounting would also have to be used for agents having a dual purpose.

In the interest of international curbs on the possibility of CW, it would appear to be wise for the United States, and for other countries, to permit a good deal of inspection of possible CW facilities by foreign nationals.

Accordingly, if other powers accept similar inspection, the United States should seek a ban on chemical weapons of the sort proposed in the United Kingdom draft convention for biological weapons. It would not be necessary to combine the two types of weapons in one convention, although there would be strong arguments for doing so now were it not for the predicament resulting from use by the United States of harassing or riot control agents and defoliants in Vietnam.

Should there be a delay in the general willingness of countries to agree to this sort of CW ban, it could be worthwhile to seek a CW test ban treaty and a treaty prohibiting proliferation in this field. There could be a ban on stockpiles of any BW or CW material outside the territorial limits of the country possessing it.

The United States should therefore prepare a proposal for

the CCD at Geneva for a total ban on the use of CW, and on manufacturing, stockpiling, and retention of manufacturing facilities, with the continued right to do research on and develop defenses against CW. There should be no exception for riot control or harassing or incapacitating agents. A ban on the training of troops for offensive CW should be included. There should be verification procedures that would be as unintrusive as possible while still permitting a high probability of detection of non-observance of the ban. The proposal might be along the lines of the British proposal on BW. At the same time, the United States should continue research to find more effective and less intrusive means of verifying compliance with a wide ban on CW and the means of waging it.

If it is impossible to obtain international agreement to a wide CW ban by means of a treaty, it might be feasible, as in the case of BW, to seek to persuade as many nations as possible to register a renunciation covering production, stockpiling, and use in retaliation as well as first use, and applying in favor of all countries, whether or not they register.

Failing any of the above, there is the possibility of encouraging as many powers as possible to take the sort of unilateral action the United States took in 1969 on BW and Canada took in 1970 on both BW and CW. There is also the possibility of seeking a United Nations resolution, which might pave the way to stronger action.

It is of course not possible to know beforehand what the reactions of other countries will be. Some countries, such as Sweden, have traditionally been prepared to accept the banning of weapons of mass destruction with minimal safeguards. Other countries have traditionally been reluctant to agree to international verification, often equating it with espionage. Still others have felt that lack of verification presented unacceptable risks to their national security. If agreement is to be reached, it will be necessary to settle on some middle ground. This has been achieved to some extent in the field of nuclear weapons in the Antarctic Treaty and in the Non-Proliferation Treaty. The latter empowers the International Atomic Energy Agency (IAEA) to verify compliance by the non-nuclear powers; the United States and the United Kingdom have offered to open their non-defense nuclear facilities to IAEA inspection and have urged other nuclear powers that are parties to the treaty to do likewise. So far, the Soviet Union has not responded. Nor have France and Mainland China, which are not parties to the treaty, indicated willingness to accept IAEA inspection.

Because of the inexorable law of development, through science and technology, of constantly more sophisticated weaponry, today is almost always better than tomorrow for an effort to limit weapons, particularly those of mass destruction. There have been impressive and depressing advances in "the state of the art" of killing or incapacitating through the use of chemical agents since their first widespread use in World War I. New means of their dissemination, as with other weapons, have supplemented conventional artillery and bombing by airplane. Today, chemical weapons are of relatively secondary importance in national arsenals, which contain so much else. The long-term effects of certain uses of chemical agents, on people and on ecology, are of general concern to civilization in peacetime, and these ill effects, not wholly predictable, add a new inhumane dimension to the possible use of chemical weapons in warfare. There are Orwellian possibilities of man's use against his enemies of his expanding ability to control the creation of human life itself. The United States should now take the lead in maintaining the momentum of arms control by proposing further CBW limitations and by seeking to obtain their general acceptance.

REFERENCES

1. *Chemical and Bacteriological (Biological) Weapons and the Effects of their Possible Use,* United Nations Pub. Sales No. E.69.I.24, p. 88, para. 375. The fourteen consultant experts who prepared the report at the request of the Secretary-General of the United Nations were Dr. Ivan L. Bennett of New York University; a Soviet academician; and specialists from Canada, Czechoslovakia, Ethiopia, France, Great Britain, Hungary, India, Japan, Mexico, The Netherlands, Poland, and Sweden.
2. *New York Times,* 19 Feb. 1970.
3. UN Doc. CCD/PV.460, 24 Mar. 1970.
4. UN Doc. CCD/255/Rev. 2, 18 Aug. 1969.
5. See pp. 113–114.
6. UN Doc. CCD/285, 14 Apr. 1970.
7. For text of the statement, see UN Doc. CCD/PV.464, 14 Apr. 1970, esp. pp. 21–22.
8. UN Doc. CCD/PV.465, 16 Apr. 1970, esp. pp. 26–30.
9. The word "control," as used by Yugoslavs and members of the Soviet bloc, has a meaning close to that of the French word "controle," which is used in the sense of "verify." It does *not* mean "to exercise control, or power, over."
10. The Swedish representative, in April 1970, had made an important speech on the CBW problem, urging careful exploration of verification possibilities before drafting of actual proposals, and reviewing the positions taken by various countries on the CBW ban. See UN Doc. CCD/PV.463, 9 Apr. 1970, pp. 5–13.
11. See pp. 108–117.
12. The different aspects of verification of compliance with the WEU ban on CW are in Protocols 3 and 4, adopted in Paris, to the Treaty of Brussels, generally referred to as the WEU Treaty (1954).
13. See pp. 80–92.
14. All Warsaw Pact members and all NATO members except the United States have ratified the Geneva Protocol, most of them reserving the right of retaliation.
15. "Nerve agents are colourless, odourless, tasteless chemicals of the same family as organophosphorus insecticides. They poison the nervous system and disrupt vital body functions. They constitute the most modern war chemicals known; they kill quickly and are more potent than are any other chemical agents (except toxins)." *Chemical and Biological (Bacteriological) Weapons,* op. cit., p. 12, para. 44.
16. See p. 101.

SELECTED BIBLIOGRAPHY

1. U.S. Congress, House, Committee on Foreign Affairs, Subcommittee

on National Security Policy and Scientific Developments, *Hearings on Chemical–Biological Warfare* (Washington, D.C.: U.S. Government Printing Office, 1970). This contains, besides important testimony, copies of the Geneva Protocol of 1925, of reservations thereto, of the United Kingdom and Warsaw Pact draft proposals of 1969, of President Nixon's statement of November 1969, and of other relevant papers.

2. U.S., Congress, Senate, Committee on Labor and Public Welfare, Special Subcommittee on National Science Foundation, *Chemical and Biological Weapons, Some Possible Approaches for Lessening the Threat and Danger,* background report prepared by the Library of Congress Legislative Reference Service (Washington: U.S. Govt. Printing Office, 1969).

3. United Nations General Assembly Official Records: 24th Session, 1969, Annexes, Agenda Item 104: "Question of chemical and bacteriological (biological) weapons."

4. Verbatim Records of the Conference of the Committee on Disarmament (at Geneva):

   a. Working Paper submitted by the United States, UN Doc. CCD/283, 16 Mar. 1970.

   b. Statement by representative of the United States, UN Doc. CCD/PV.458, 17 Mar. 1970.

   c. Statement by representative of Canada, UN Doc. CCD/PV.460, 24 Mar. 1970.

   d. Statement by representative of Sweden, UN Doc. CCD/PV.463, 9 Apr. 1970.

   e. Working Paper submitted by Hungary, Mongolia, and Poland, UN Doc. CCD/285, 14 Apr. 1970.

   f. Statement by representative of Poland, UN Doc. CCD/PV.464, 14 Apr. 1970.

   g. Statement by representative of Yugoslavia, UN Doc. CCD/PV. 465, 16 Apr. 1970.

5. "Escalation of Chemical Warfare," *New Scientist* (London), 14 Aug. 1969.

6. Meselson, Matthew S. "Behind the Nixon Policy for Chemical and Biological Warfare," *Science and Public Affairs: Bulletin of the Atomic Scientists,* Jan. 1970.

7. Whiteside, Thomas. "A Reporter at Large: Defoliation," *New Yorker,* 7 Feb. 1970.

8. "Nixon's Report to Congress on Foreign Policy," *The New York Times,* 19 Feb. 1970.

9. "U.S. Shows Sign of Concern Over Effect of 9–Year Defoliation Program in Vietnam," *The New York Times,* 15 Mar. 1970.

10. Meselson, Matthew S. "Chemical and Biological Weapons," *Scientific American,* May 1970.

COMMENTS

George Bunn
Former General Counsel, Arms Control and Disarmament Agency

I will limit my comments to the legal problems of interpretation of the Geneva Protocol because that is the area where I have particular competence. In my view, the language and negotiating history of the Protocol do *not clearly show* that it prohibits the use of tear gas and chemical defoliants in war. The paper on the "Legal Aspects of the Geneva Protocol" overstates the case for such an interpretation. First, it begins by assuming that the Protocol's language "asphyxiating, poisonous or other gases" should be read "asphyxiating, poisonous or *all* other gases" rather than "asphyxiating, poisonous or *similar* other gases." Since lawyers and courts often draw meaning for a word like "other" from companion words like "poisonous and asphyxiating," I believe "similar other" to be as likely a plain meaning as "all other."

Second, having begun with the premise that the language clearly prohibits tear gases and chemical defoliants, the paper infers that parties to the Protocol which have never taken a contrary view of its meaning must now be assumed to have accepted this one. In my experience, countries often fail to disagree without intending to be bound by their silence. This seems particularly true in this case when a report of a conference called to resolve the differences of view indicated that agreement could not be reached.[1] On the other hand, the over-

---

1. See Bunn, "Banning Poison Gas and Germ Warfare: Should the United States Agree?" *Wisconsin Law Review,* Vol. 375 (1969), p. 408.

whelming majority of countries which recently expressed themselves in the United Nations on this subject appear to be of the view that tear gases and chemical defoliants are barred by the Protocol. While very many of the allies of the United States abstained on this vote, it is nevertheless the best indication available of current national views on the scope of the Protocol.

I believe that the manner in which these agents are actually now used in Viet Nam by the United States cannot be supported by the justification which was given to the world when that use began: that these agents would be used to save lives and in a manner similar to their use to control riots or kill weeds at home.[2]

In my view, the future United States position on whether tear gases and chemical defoliants are to be banned should depend primarily on a realistic appraisal of the advantages and disadvantages of the use of these agents in the future, not on the legal history of the Protocol. In that appraisal I would weigh not only the military experience gained in Viet Nam but also the risk of future escalation to more dangerous chemicals if other countries become experienced in the use of tear gases and defoliants simply because we insist upon holding open loopholes for their use.

Paul Doty
Professor of Chemistry, Harvard University

Historians of the future, sensitive to the way man's destiny is shaped by the way he uses his ever-expanding scientific talents, will surely give prominence to two parallel but strikingly antagonistic developments of the 1960's: herbicide warfare and the green revolution. Each represents a dramatic extension of man's control into the plant world, the essential link between the energy of the sun and human habitation on earth that makes human society possible. Prudently used, the green revolution can provide that necessary margin of time in which

---

2. Ibid., pp. 405-406, 408-409.

world population control can be humanely achieved. Unleashing the full potential of herbicide warfare, of which only the beginning has been seen in Vietnam, can provide a new dimension to warfare, eliminate plant life in vast areas of the world and damage the gene pool with the consequent increased burden of defective offspring.

These possibilities are only on the horizon and no one can predict when they might become reality—it depends on too many uncertain factors and human choices. But our vastly increased comprehension of life processes, and with this the recognition of thousands of new vital connections in living systems at which fatal interdiction is possible at a very low dose level insures the discovery of a succession of more diverse and effective herbicides. With predictable growth also in the techniques and capability of dispersal, one can foresee in a vague but terrifying way the consequences of persistent, unrestrained, large scale development of herbicide warfare by the end of this century.

It is understandable that this sense of scale and long term future has not been the focus of the papers in this volume. There is so much that is here and now and requires analysis in order to chart our immediate future that one is uninclined to divert his attention to the shadowy and indistinct forms of a distant future. But when the impact of the Vietnam experience in herbicide warfare has been absorbed and the diplomatic and military and human consequences assessed, this vision of the possible future must inform the decisions that are taken, the path that this country will choose. One path requires a halt to our present practice of herbicide warfare and our further development of the technique, and that we join with the great majority of nations who clearly want this new and ultimately self-destructive activity banished. The other path leads by stages to the dedication of the innovative skill and industry of this nation, augmented by the certain expansion of the scientific basis on which such work rests, to an unending assault upon the life support system of this planet. A whole society, conscious of its leadership role, cannot at the same time invest its resources in the green revolution and herbicide warfare.

Judge Philip Jessup
Former Justice of the International Court of Justice

As a member of the Chemical and Biological Warfare Study Group, I should like to express my agreement with the conclusions of the paper "Limitations on CBW Going Beyond Those of the Geneva Protocol" by Archibald S. Alexander and in the paper entitled "The Military Value and Political Implications of the Use of Riot Control Agents in Warfare." Those recommendations would support the policy enunciated by President Nixon last November, and if strongly espoused by the United States would begin to counteract the damage to our national position caused by the delay in pressing for Senate consent to ratification of the Geneva Protocol.

I favor alternative No. 7 in the paper "Legal Aspects of the Geneva Protocol of 1925" by Baxter and Buergenthal, that is, the requesting of an advisory opinion from the International Court of Justice. As they suggest, the United States in pressing for such a request should state in advance that it would accept as decisive the Court's opinion. This precedent acceptance would be the same as that in the Convention on the Privileges and Immunities of the United Nations which the United States at long last has ratified. This course of action would be in accordance with the sound policy in such matters of avoiding the burden of unilateralism.

The fact that the Security Council on 29 July 1970 adopted (for the first time in its history) a resolution requesting the Court to give an advisory opinion, suggests that the effort to secure such an opinion on the interpretation of the Geneva Protocol should be launched in the Security Council.

Robert W. Komer
Former United States Ambassador in charge of the Pacification Program in Vietnam

As a long time student, analyst, and partisan of constructive arms control measures, I join vigorously in supporting any proposals which make demonstrable sense in a still volatile world. CBW emphatically falls in this category, because its mass use can have horrendous side effects on innocent civilians, while it has proven over the years of only marginal security value—especially in a nuclear age. At the same time, I regret that some of the harsh criticism of CBW seems overstated and impressionistic without sufficient firm basis in hard evidence. It may be true, but the fact is we just do not know.

In this category lie many of the contentions about the adverse consequences of the use of herbicides in Vietnam, which I had occasion to observe firsthand during my tour of duty there. There is little question that use (or misuse) of herbicides had many counterproductive effects, while in at least one case —that of crop destruction agents—it accomplished little if anything. But some critics have gone on to make assertions that are so obviously biassed, and so thinly based as to raise questions about their scientific objectivity. For example, accusations have been made about the destruction of the ecological balance in Vietnam with far too little attention to in-depth investigation over time. Even wilder charges have been made about the deliberate use of herbicides to force the South Vietnamese civilian population into the cities from the countryside. This just is not so.

While such excess by no means characterizes the views expressed by the knowledgeable Carnegie panelist on this painful subject, David Brown, it so dominates the debate over use of herbicides in Vietnam that I wish to take this opportunity to make a plea for more dispassionate analysis and less passionate conjecture. It is essential that we know whereof we speak if we are to make the best case for lasting arms control.

APPENDIX

Geneva Protocol of 1925

Protocol for the Prohibition of the Use in War of Asphyxiating, Poisonous or Other Gases, and of Bacteriological Methods of Warfare

The undersigned Plenipotentiaries, in the name of their respective Governments:

Whereas the use in war of asphyxiating, poisonous or other gases, and of all analogous liquids, materials or devices, has been justly condemned by the general opinion of the civilised world; and

Whereas the prohibition of such use has been declared in Treaties to which the majority of Powers of the world are Parties; and

To the end that this prohibition shall be universally accepted as a part of International Law, binding alike the conscience and the practice of nations;

Declare:

That the High Contracting Parties, so far as they are not already Parties to Treaties prohibiting such use, accept this prohibition, agree to extend this prohibition to the use of bacteriological methods of warfare and agree to be bound as between themselves according to the terms of this declaration.

The High Contracting Parties will exert every effort to induce other States to accede to the present Protocol. Such accession will be notified to the Government of the French Republic, and by the latter to all signatory and acceding Powers, and will take effect on the date of the notification by the Government of the French Republic.

The present Protocol, of which the French and English texts are both authentic, shall be ratified as soon as possible. It shall bear today's date.

The ratifications of the present Protocol shall be addressed to the Government of the French Republic, which will at once notify the deposit of such ratification to each of the signatory and acceding Powers.

The instruments of ratification of and accession to the present Protocol will remain deposited in the archives of the Government of the French Republic.

The present Protocol will come into force for each signatory Power as from the date of deposit of its ratification, and, from that moment, each Power will be bound as regards other Powers which have already deposited their ratifications.

In witness whereof the Plenipotentiaries have signed the present Protocol.

Done at Geneva in a single copy, this seventeenth day of June, One Thousand Nine Hundred and Twenty-Five.

United Kingdom Draft Convention

Revised Draft Convention for the Prohibition
of Biological Methods of Warfare

The States concluding this Convention, hereinafter referred to as the "Parties to the Convention",

Recalling that many States have become Parties to The Protocol for the Prohibition of the Use in War of Asphyxiating, Poisonous or other Gases, and of Bacteriological Methods of Warfare, signed at Geneva on 17 June 1925,

Recognising the contribution that the said Protocol has already made, and continues to make, to mitigating the horrors of war,

Recalling further United Nations General Assembly Resolutions 2162 B (XXI) of 5 December, 1966, and 2454 A (XXIII) of 20 December, 1968, which called for strict observance by all States of the principles and objectives of the Geneva Protocol and invited all States to accede to it,

Believing that chemical and biological discoveries should be used only for the betterment of human life,

Recognising nevertheless that the development of scientific knowledge throughout the world will increase the risk of eventual use of biological methods of warfare,

Convinced that such use would be repugnant to the conscience of mankind and that no effort should be spared to minimise this risk,

Desiring therefore to reinforce the Geneva Protocol by the conclusion of a Convention making special provision in this field,

Declaring their belief that, in particular, provision should be made for the prohibition of recourse to biological methods of warfare in any circumstances,

Have agreed as follows:

Article I

Each of the Parties to the Convention undertakes, insofar as it may not already be committed in that respect under Treaties or other instruments in force prohibiting the use of chemical and biological methods of warfare, never in any circumstances, by making use for hostile purposes of microbial or other biological agents causing death, damage or disease by infection or infestation to man, other animals, or crops, to engage in biological methods of warfare.

Article II

Each of the Parties to the Convention undertakes:

(a) not to produce or otherwise acquire, or assist in or permit the production or acquisition of:

(i) microbial or other biological agents of types and in quantities that have no independent justification for prophylactic or other peaceful purposes;

(ii) ancillary equipment or vectors the purpose of which is to facilitate the use of such agents for hostile purposes;

(b) not to conduct, assist or permit research aimed at production of the kind prohibited in sub-paragraph (a) of this Article; and

(c) to destroy, or divert to peaceful purposes, within three months after the Convention comes into force for that Party, any stocks in its possession of such agents or ancillary equipment or vectors as have been produced or otherwise acquired for hostile purposes.

Article III

1. Any Party to the Convention which believes that biological methods of warfare have been used against it may lodge a complaint with the Secretary-General of the United Nations, submitting all evidence at its disposal in support of the complaint, and request that the complaint be investigated and that a report on the result of the investigation be submitted to the Security Council.

2. Any Party to the Convention which believes that another Party has acted in breach of its undertaking under Articles I and II of the Convention, but which is not entitled to lodge a complaint under Paragraph I of this Article, may lodge a complaint with the Security Council, submitting all evidence at its disposal, and request that the complaint be investigated.

3. Each of the Parties to the Convention undertakes to co-operate fully with the Secretary-General and his authorised representatives in any investigation he may carry out, as a result of a complaint, in accordance with Security Council Resolution No. ——.[1]

Article IV

Each of the Parties to the Convention affirms its intention to provide or support appropriate assistance, in accordance with the United Nations Charter, to any Party to the Convention, if the Security Council concludes that biological methods of warfare have been used against that Party.

Article V

Each of the Parties to the Convention undertakes to pursue negotiations in good faith on effective measures to strengthen the existing constraints on chemical methods of warfare.

---

[1] A draft Security Council resolution attached in the U.K. draft convention is not printed here.

Article VI

Nothing contained in the present Convention shall be construed as in any way limiting or derogating from obligations assumed by any State under the Protocol for the Prohibition of the Use in War of Asphyxiating, Poisonous or other Gases, and of Bacteriological Methods of Warfare, signed at Geneva on 17 June, 1925.

Article VII

[Provisions for amendments.]

Article VIII

[Provisions for Signature, Ratification, Entry into Force, etc.]

Article IX

1. This Convention shall be of unlimited duration.

2. Each Party shall in exercising its national sovereignty have the right to withdraw from the Convention, if it decides that extraordinary events, related to the subject matter of this Convention, have jeopardised the supreme interests of its country. It shall give notice of such withdrawal to all other Parties to the Convention and to the United Nations Security Council three months in advance. Such notice shall include a statement of the extraordinary events it regards as having jeopardised its supreme interests.

Article X

[Provisions on languages of text, etc.]

Statement by President Nixon

White House press release dated 25 November 1969.

Soon after taking office I directed a comprehensive study of our chemical and biological defense policies and programs. There had been no such review in over 15 years. As a result, objectives and policies in this field were unclear and programs lacked definition and direction.

Under the auspices of the National Security Council, the Departments of State and Defense, the Arms Control and Disarmament Agency, the Office of Science and Technology, the intelligence community, and other agencies worked closely together on this study for over 6 months. These government efforts were aided by contributions from the scientific community through the President's Scientific Advisory Committee.

This study has now been completed and its findings carefully considered by the National Security Council. I am now reporting the decisions taken on the basis of this review.

Chemical Warfare Program

As to our chemical warfare program, the United States:

—Reaffirms its oft-repeated renunciation of the first use of lethal chemical weapons.

—Extends this renunciation to the first use of incapacitating chemicals. Consonant with these decisions, the administration will submit to the Senate, for its advice and consent to ratification, the Geneva protocol of 1925, which prohibits the first use in war of "asphyxiating, poisonous or other gases and of bacteriological methods of warfare." The United States has long supported the principles and objectives of this protocol. We take this step toward formal ratification to reinforce our continuing advocacy of international constraints on the use of these weapons.

Biological Research Program

Biological weapons have massive, unpredictable, and potentially uncontrollable consequences. They may produce global epidemics and impair the health of future generations. I have therefore decided that:

—The United States shall renounce the use of lethal biological agents and weapons and all other methods of biological warfare.

—The United States will confine its biological research to defensive measures, such as immunization and safety measures.

—The Department of Defense has been asked to make recommendations as to the disposal of existing stocks of bacteriological weapons.

In the spirit of these decisions, the United States associates itself with the principles and objectives of the United Kingdom draft convention, which would ban the use of biological methods of warfare. We will seek, however, to clarify specific provisions of the draft to assure that necessary safeguards are included.

President Nixon's Message

White House press release dated 19 August 1970.
To the Senate of the United States:

With a view to receiving the advice and consent of the Senate to ratification, I transmit herewith the Protocol for the Prohibition of the Use in War of Asphyxiating, Poisonous or Other Gases, and of Bacteriological Methods of Warfare, signed at Geneva June 17, 1925.[1] I transmit also the report by the Secretary of State which sets forth the understandings and the proposed reservation of the United States with respect to the Protocol.

In submitting this Protocol for approval, I consider it desirable and appropriate to make the following statements:

—The United States has renounced the first-use of lethal and incapacitating chemical weapons.

—The United States has renounced any use of biological and toxin weapons.

—Our biological and toxin programs will be confined to research for defensive purposes, strictly defined. By the example we set, we hope to contribute to an atmosphere of peace, understanding and confidence between nations and among men. The policy of the United States Government is to support international efforts to limit biological and toxin research programs to defensive purposes.

—The United States will seek further agreement on effective arms-control measures in the field of biological and chemical warfare.

Today, there are 85 parties, including all other major powers, to this basic international agreement which the United States proposed and signed in 1925. The United States always has observed the principles and objectives of this Protocol.

I consider it essential that the United States now become a party to this Protocol, and urge the Senate to give its advice and consent to ratification with the reservation set forth in the Secretary's report.

Richard Nixon

The White House,
August 19, 1970.

PB-34309
5-14